Murder & Crime
STRATFORD-UPON-AVON

Murder & Crime
STRATFORD-UPON-AVON

NICK BILLINGHAM

The
History
Press

This book is dedicated to Nick Billingham, our father, a proud 'Stratfordian' who was a very interesting and honourable man.

Victoria and Amber Billingham

Nick died in April 2009 before this book was published.

Frontispiece: There's much more to Stratford's history than Shakespeare. There has always been agriculture and industry, and, of course, lots of crime.

First published 2009

The History Press
The Mill, Brimscombe Port
Stroud, Gloucestershire, GL5 2QG
www.thehistorypress.co.uk

British Library Cataloguing in Publication Data.
A catalogue record for this book is available from the British Library.

ISBN 978 0 7524 5168 8

Typesetting and origination by The History Press
Printed in Great Britain

CONTENTS

ACKNOWLEDGEMENTS

Special thanks are due to the staff of the Shakespeare Birthplace Trust Records Office and Warwickshire County Library for all their assistance. Also to my wife for putting up with papers and text all over the place during the writing of this and for her constant encouragement.

INTRODUCTION

The town of Stratford is world famous for Shakespeare. We have theatres, the birthplace, stacks of touristy shops selling busts of the Bard and all the other essentials of a thriving industry. In some respects this is a shame because the town has so much more to offer our visitors. Shakespeare is just one of the characters who have helped mould the history and character of the town over the centuries. There have been the thousands of citizens, each of whom has played a small part in making Stratford such a pleasant little market town. We're not all playwrights; there have been butchers and bakers, rich merchants and poor farmers. There have been saints and sinners. This book deals with the sinners.

The stories in the town's history have always been important. Shakespeare himself had been brought up with the local stories and legends and used these as inspiration as he wove them into the plots of his plays. It's always the goriest stories that last the longest. In the year that Shakespeare was born, Charlotte Clopton was supposed to have been entombed in the family vault whilst she was still alive. A week later, the vault was re-opened for another burial and the shocked funeral party discovered that Charlotte had awoken in her coffin, struggled out and tried to escape from the pitch dark vault. They found her still standing, her fingers stuck in a crevice in the stone work, stone dead. She had bitten into her own shoulder in a delirium of thirst. Such a grisly tale is reputed to have inspired the tomb scene in *Romeo and Juliet*. Another local legend, again from the Clopton family, is that of Margaret Clopton. She was passionately in love with a young man, who wasn't quite so keen on her, and dumped

> WIFE MURDER AT COVENTRY.—*Frederick King*, a grey-haired weaver, aged 48, was indicted for the murder of his wife, Eliza King, at Coventry, on the 5th of May.—Mr. Adams appeared for the prosecution; the prisoner conducted his own defence.—On Sunday the 4th of May, a quarrel took place between prisoner and deceased, in consequence of his wife neglecting to cook some mackrel. Deceased, it was stated

Life in Victorian Warwickshire was chronicled in the *Warwickshire Advertiser* in all its gory detail.

her. Margaret was so distraught that she completely lost the plot and chucked herself down the well. She was destined to become the role model for Ophelia in *Hamlet*.

In a world without television and radio, stories around the fireplace were the main entertainment, but even today, if you listen carefully to the conversations in the local pubs, there are tales of the old local murders, dodgy deeds in the villages, of how things used to be. It is an unchanging feature of our lives; the oral traditions of the town find their way from generation to generation not from any historical imperative, but because they are cracking good tales. The stories are all about those dramatic moments in the town's life and their themes are the eternal ones of lust and anger, greed and jealousy.

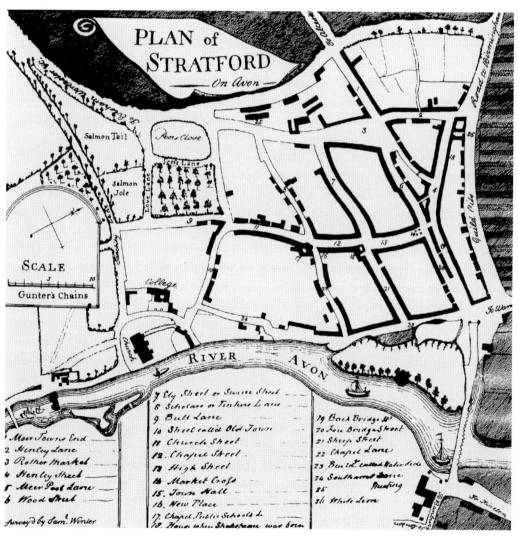

The first map of Stratford in 1765 shows a small little market town of only a few thousand souls.

Shakespeare has dominated the town since 1769, but behind the tourist image life carries on as normal.

So here we have 400 years of how murders and crime have played their part in Stratford's history. It's all a long way from traditional local history, but more immediate for all of that. For the most part no one gives a hoot about the Corn Laws, but the way that they reduced the farm workers to a life of poverty and crime, well there's another story. In most cases murders are very easily solved – the spouse is found still clutching a bloodstained poker muttering that that was the last time they played away.

Stratford is peculiarly well-endowed with some very odd and unsolved cases. The Meon Hill murder remains an almost archetypal case, and the real facts now lie almost buried amidst a welter of superstition and misinformation. The case of Olive Bennett, the nurse strangled in the churchyard, is another one, although probably with a somewhat more mundane explanation. The strange tale of Johan von Gamsenfells is an equally bizarre story, although far less well known. Perhaps it was madness, perhaps international espionage and intrigue. It is certainly a most peculiar incident.

Madness itself has led to murder. After researching over 200 cases for my various books on crime, it stands out as such a random bolt from the blue. Luckily for Stratford it hasn't featured, but it has in nearby towns and I have taken the liberty of examining a couple of cases that strike me as very distinctive. If ever there was something to send a chill shiver of horror down your spine, these cases are the ones.

Quite a few townsfolk have ended up in the cemetery unexpectedly early.

The cases in this book end about fifty years ago. This isn't because the locals have all become angels overnight; far from it, they are still just as murderous as ever. It is because the cases are still fresh, not only in the town's folklore, but in the memories of the people directly involved; people who have lost relatives and friends. It is not the intention of this book to add to their suffering. Once the years have passed and history has eased the grief then a new generation of historians can examine them. In the meantime, you can learn from history just how similar to us our ancestors really were, and how precarious life can be.

CHAPTER ONE

———◆◆◆———

CRIME IN SHAKESPEARE'S STRATFORD

'He will spoil my father'

Stratford is famous because of William Shakespeare. Students and professors pore over the old plays trying to learn what influences helped to create one of the world's literary giants. Luckily for us the archive at the Shakespeare Centre preserves not only the plays but much of the early history of the town, including what remains of the records of everyday life when the playwright was alive. Alas in 400 years much has disappeared; bits of paper vanish off my desk overnight, so you can guess how much has been lost in four centuries. Stratford itself underwent a huge upheaval in the years just before Shakespeare was born; the Reformation closed down the old Catholic guilds that ran the town, and for seven years there was no local government at all. A whole new order was created in 1553 when the new Borough was created. The townspeople were still the same though, and just as likely to break the law. The world that Shakespeare grew up in might have had a new government, but human nature was unchanged.

Shakespeare frequently parodied the pompous and vain aldermen of the town. They were a pretty self-important bunch of the town's wealthiest merchants. It wasn't exactly an arduous job, lording over the other shopkeepers, making sure that the lord of the manor was kept sweet and organising the ale tasting. Top of the pile of the Borough Council was the Mayor, elected by the other burgesses each year. It was such a cushy job you would not expect it to get a mention in a book like this, and yet during Shakespeare's lifetime one of our mayors died in office, brutally stabbed.

Thomas Waterman, alias Dixon, was elected Mayor for 1608. He came from a large family and one of his relatives, Richard, ran the Swan pub at the bottom of Bridge Street. Today it is known as the Encore. The surviving records are a bit patchy to say the least, but it seems his family were very wealthy and owned a considerable amount of property in the town. In 1603, one of his relatives, also a Thomas, died and as a result we know a lot about the pub from his will. It was one of the most prestigious in the town with several reception rooms and parlours, all well-furnished.

In 1608 the Encore was known as the Swan and was one of the biggest inns in the town.

On the night of 22 April, life was pottering on much as usual in the Swan. In the inner parlour Thomas Waterman and Humphrey Acton were sitting each side of the fireplace, chatting over this and that. Thomas needed to keep in touch with all the gossip so he could keep his finger on the political pulse. Life in Stratford may have been unutterably dull in those days, but the political and judicial machinations of the aldermen were notorious. They were forever trying to catch each other out in some petty way. If you missed church, opened your shop or pub on a Sunday, committed adultery, anything was grist to the gossip mill and often ended up in front of the Church Court. Humphrey and Thomas were deep in conversation, whilst next door in the main bar his relative Richard was on duty, together with his wife and two daughters. It seems that the only other person in that bar was Lewes Gilberte, a local butcher, and he was getting the beer down his throat with gusto. His wife, Christiana, had been up in front of the Church Court some months before and perhaps it was this that was preying on his mind.

No one ever recorded what actually started the argument. After a few beers it was probably something utterly trivial. Richard ordered Lewes Gilberte to get out of the pub. He wasn't going to go and Richard tried to manhandle him out. A fight promptly started and Richard wasn't getting the best of it. Lewes Gilberte drew out a long knife. Richard's wife screamed, and his daughter yelled for help,

'He will spoil my father, he will murder my father!' The shrieks rang out across the street.

Thomas Waterman got up from the cosy seat by the fireplace and went to the door of the parlour. On the other side Richard and Lewes were grappling together and at first Thomas couldn't push the door open. After a massive heave the door burst open and Thomas rushed to his relative's aid. He grabbed Lewes Gilberte by the collar of his doublet and started to push him towards the front door.

Lewes rounded on him, plunging the wickedly long and sharp butcher's knife into his stomach. The blade went right in, a couple of inches to the right of his navel and all the way up to the hilt. Thomas gasped and sagged to the floor.

Thomas Waterman was sitting quietly by this very fireplace.

Lewis Gilberte would have been held in the town's lock-up next to the town hall.

Stratford was a quiet place in those days; the girls' screams had alerted everyone in the whole of Bridge Street and beyond. Within moments Lewes Gilberte was overpowered by neighbours and held under arrest. It was all too late for Thomas Waterman. He was bleeding internally from the massive gash and gradually weakened through the rest of the evening, finally dying not long after midnight. His career as Mayor had been brought to an untimely end.

The records are silent about what happened to Lewes Gilberte. So many have gone missing over the years, both in the town's archive and that of the county. The inquest a couple of days later decided that Thomas Waterman, alias Dixon, had been wilfully murdered by Lewes Gilberte. At that point Gilberte would have been moved from the town's lock-up and taken to Warwick to be held prisoner until the next Assizes. The chances are that he was then hanged, but those records are missing too.

The murder was one of the most dramatic of crimes during Shakespeare's lifetime, but by no means the only one. In 1605, Guy Fawkes and other conspirators tried to blow up Parliament, and Clopton House, just to the north of the town, was one of their 'safe houses'. Our local plotter was one Ambrose Rockwood. He was a rather dozy young man whose passion in life was horse racing. He did a bit of wheeler-dealing on the side; indeed one of his best deals was selling a large amount of cheap gunpowder to a bloke called Robert Catesby. Catesby was already involved in the conspiracy to blow up Parliament and at the end of 1604 invited Ambrose to join in the plot to destroy the government and set up a new Catholic administration. England had been through two generations of religious strife, but still the factions were deeply divided. In the towns and cities the new Protestant way of life was settling down, but out in the country the old Catholic faith was as strong as ever. As the balance of power swung first one way and then the other, most people just kept their heads down and hoped for a quiet life. Martyrs were created on both sides in a welter of sectarian violence that should have provided the rest of history with a lesson never to be forgotten. Somehow the commandment about killing seems to have been overlooked by both sides and those who don't learn from history are destined to repeat it.

Ambrose Rockwood rented Clopton House in early 1605 and set about turning it into a safe house, complete with underground tunnels and even a chapel dug beneath the cellars. Of course he didn't actually do all the digging himself, what were the farm labourers for? It is quite probable that everyone in the town knew what was going on from their gossip. The way of the world at the time was to let the Catholics get on with their worship privately, and once in a while have a bit of a purge, fining them for recusancy. It was effectively a tax, and like all other taxes the system was designed to let them keep just enough to go on until you taxed them again. It gradually reduced the old Catholic families to penury.

Ambrose Rockwood prepared Clopton House to be one of the centres of rebellion once the explosion had taken place in London. On 31 October he rode down to London to meet up with Guy Fawkes and the others to get ready for the big bang. He was as clueless as the rest of them about just how far their plot had been compromised. Indeed, there is even one theory that the gunpowder that he had managed to pick up so cheap was so degraded that it could never have actually exploded, and that the government spies were fully aware of this. The conspirators met up in anticipation of the grand rebellion, confident that all of England would rally to their cause and the Old Faith. At the meeting, Ambrose was presented with an ornamental sword engraved with the prayer of the Passion of Christ. Even as the sword was handed over, officers of the watch were arresting Guy Fawkes. All across London the plotters were being arrested. Most of the real players were already flying for their lives. Dozy old Ambrose was the last to discover that the plot had been uncovered. He leapt on his horse and fled with only minutes to spare.

He may have been a bit of a berk, but he was one hell of a horseman. He managed to catch up with the other plotters on their way back towards Warwickshire, even though they had had a day's start on him. It all went a bit downhill from there though. They couldn't rendezvous at Clopton House. By the time the party had got to Warwick, word had already reached Stratford and the townspeople had raced up to the house and searched it, uncovering all the secret passages and chapel. In much the same way, they had to avoid Coughton Court near Alcester and ended up spending the night at Hewell Grange. A clear measure of just how dozy Ambrose was – he decided to dry out their stock of gunpowder in front of an open fire.

The resulting explosion blinded Ambrose and alerted the local militia. In the resulting gun fight, Ambrose was wounded and then arrested. The rest, as they say, is history. He was taken to London, tried and then hung, drawn and quartered. It wasn't a good way to die. As he was drawn through the streets on a hurdle he saw his young wife in the crowd, 'Pray for me', he begged.

For the most part, life in Shakespeare's Stratford was pretty quiet. It was only a small market town of about 2,000 souls. The justice system consisted of two parts; the secular and the church. There were plenty of secular crimes to commit, from selling short measures to leaving piles of manure in the street and letting ferocious dogs roam at large, and the Borough records are full of these relatively trivial offences. Serious crime was very rare and was dealt with at the Assizes in Warwick, so it doesn't feature in the town's records. The Church Court was where the real scandals and gossip came to light. The court was under the jurisdiction of the Bishop of Worcester, although for the most part it was exercised by the local vicar and his cronies. Since everyone had to be a member of the church, everyone was subject to it. The vicar made sure that no one strayed from the path of righteousness.

The vicar of Stratford held the Bawdy Court in the church.

Quite a few of the Church Court's records survive and they give us a fascinating glimpse into Shakespeare's world. Not the slightest thing missed the beady eye of the vicar; the town had enough gossips to make sure of that. The system may well have survived for centuries, even through the Reformation, but it doesn't seem to have made the citizens any better people. The same old frailties just kept coming up before the court.

If you thought today's world is a bit loose on the old morals, well think again. In sixteenth-century Stratford they were at it like rabbits. Time and again people were hauled up before the court for adultery or sexual incontinence. The vicar, John Rogers, seems to have had a bit of a blitz on the loose morals of the town in 1606. The February session of the Church Court was packed. First in front of the bench was Bartholomew Parsons. He had been privately interrogated by the vicar in his house and admitted having an affair with the widow Alice Attwood. There wasn't much he could do to deny it, she was now eight months pregnant. He was ordered to do the public penance of standing in church wearing a white sheet for two Sunday services. This was sufficiently humiliating for him to offer to pay a fine of 10s and stand wearing his own clothes rather than the white sheet. The vicar decided to take the money and let him be. The problem for the vicar was that Alice Attwood had been caught with Richard Burman too, and neither Alice or Richard had bothered to turn up at the court. They were both excommunicated. Richard was then accused of bedding Anne Attwood as well. Busy lad!

Next before the vicar was Anne Ward, who was accused of a relationship with Daniel Baker. Once again, she was pregnant and Daniel didn't turn up at court. She said that he had promised to marry her, but still had to do the public penance a month later. Poor old Margery Mills didn't even know who the father of her child was so she didn't even bother coming to court. Anne Wood was then arraigned, also for going to bed with Daniel Baker. John Tybbottes then had to admit he had been more than a little friendly with Joan Francklyn. Edward Latymer was then accused by four people of having 'carnal copulation with a certain woman'. He said this was defamation and would produce his wife Elizabeth and Francis Horneby to testify for him. This doesn't seem to have done the trick and the case notes end: 'Latymer fled and the others were dismissed'.

Maybe it all ended up happily; Bartholomew's daughter Anna was baptised a week later and Anne Ward did indeed get married that summer, although to John Perkyns not Daniel Baker. By that time there were another half-dozen cases waiting to be tried.

If a baby was born within about seven months of the wedding then there was going to be trouble. This was a bit tough really; in those days a man really needed to know that his prospective bride was fertile. If she wasn't then there was no way he could divorce her and his family line could die out. The surest way of finding out if she was fertile was also the most enjoyable way and a lot of very hastily arranged weddings were the result. Even our beloved bard got married in a hurry, and the kiddies arrived a lot earlier than the usual nine months. If you were found guilty of 'incontinence before

Some views of the town have barely changed in 400 years.

marriage' the court tended to be slightly more lenient; if nothing else the promise of betrothal was considered almost as important as the actual wedding.

Drunkenness is probably the next most regular offence, closely followed by breaking the Sabbath. Once again the offender had to make penance, though usually by paying a fine, probably because the details were far more boring than the adulterers. Of course not everyone thought that the church should have such sweeping authoritarian powers and grumbled incessantly. If you didn't pay your fines or do penance then the result could be dire indeed. Excommunication might not sound too awful today, but in Elizabethan England it meant that you couldn't do business with anyone, shouldn't even go into anyone's house. It was a complete social exclusion order and almost everyone eventually paid up their fines just to be able to buy food and sell their goods. Where it worked most effectively was against suspected Catholics and the Church Court was a powerful means of controlling them.

Perhaps not surprisingly, the idea of the Church Court gradually fell by the wayside. Even the vicars were preaching that every man was equal in the eyes of God, and that implied that the vicar had no right to judge his neighbour. As the seventeenth century wore on, the numbers of contempt of court cases went up and the whole thing was nicknamed 'the Bawdy Court'. By the eighteenth century the system was in complete collapse and today the Church Court is an anachronism reserved for the clergy alone; we've got daytime television instead.

CHAPTER TWO

THE LIFE AND WORK OF CONSTABLE JOHN ASHFIELD

Life in Stratford pottered on through the seventeenth and eighteenth century without any great fuss, apart from a civil war and the opening of the river to navigation. The town remained a quiet little agricultural market; there was little documented crime of any great drama. The town was a pretty stagnant place; the population remained at a couple of thousand whilst other Midlands towns started to grow. Things started to liven up with the first Shakespeare Jubilee in 1769, but it wasn't until the Napoleonic Wars that the age-old institutions of the town started to feel the pressure of the modern world. The French Revolution sent shockwaves through the whole of Europe and even sleepy old Stratford could not ignore the ripples.

For all the fond nostalgia for past times, if you were poor in Georgian England life was very tough, and the social hierarchy meant you were supposed to be kept in your place. The rich man was in his castle, and the poor man was still at his gate, although sometimes with the rest of the mob. If things got a little out of hand, the militia would be called out. In 1795 the Dragoons billeted in the town, ostensibly to defend us against the French, went on a drunken rampage and ended up in an all-out brawl with the locals. Three troopers butchered Joseph Pinfield in his own garden as his wife stood by screaming for mercy. The matter was investigated by the local magistrates, but it seems that the guilty men were spirited away by the Army and never satisfactorily brought to justice. A couple of rather dubious confessions were wrung out of two of the soldiers, but there's no record of them being tried at the Assizes for what was a horrific murder. Christmas 1795 was not the happiest in the town's history.

The relationship between the State, the town worthies and the ordinary working people of Warwickshire came under increasing pressure in the first decades of the nineteenth century. It was a time of increasing lawlessness and vicious punishments. Long-term imprisonment was not an option in those days, so criminals tended to be transported or hanged. The policing of the town remained in the hands of just two constables and the Justice of the Peace, as it had done for centuries.

Joseph Pinfield was brutally hacked to death in Meer Street.

In the middle of the rising tension was John Ashfield, a town constable since around 1820. He was brought up in the Falcon Inn, which his father Robert leased. John's career got off to a good start with the arrest of a gang of highwaymen. Throughout the summer of 1820 the roads around Stratford were getting more and more dangerous to travel. On the road to Warwick, several people had been brutally mugged. One chap had even been stripped naked and left for dead. Rumours were rife as to whether it was one gang or several. The whole countryside was getting increasingly restive as the farm workers were reduced to starving poverty by the recession following the war with France. Soldiers had come back from the fighting only to find that whilst they had been away their old rights to the local common land had been stripped away, local woods fenced off and booby trapped with guns and their wages reduced to subsistence level. It was getting to the stage where travelling alone on the roads was courting disaster if you were rich.

In this climate of anarchy it was only a matter of time before tragedy struck. At dawn on Sunday 5 November William Hiron was discovered lying in a ditch with massive head injuries. John Ashfield was called out to the scene of the crime and soon discovered that the assault had taken place at Littleham Bridge on the Wellesbourne Road, a mile from where William was found. There was a pool of blood in the middle of the road and signs of a brutal struggle. William's horse had found its own way back to his house in Alveston during the night. John Ashfield found no clues as to who the gang were at the scene, but he had his suspicions. William Hiron rallied a little once they got him home, enough to say, 'three villains' but then he lapsed into a coma. He had the most horrendous head injuries, with the bones smashed inwards as though hit by a sledgehammer.

One prime suspect was a petty criminal by the name of Thomas Heytrey. The rumours were that he had some bad blood in him. His sister had been hung at Warwick that April after being found guilty of cutting the throat of her mistress at Dial House Farm. Ann Heytrey insisted that she had no idea what strange mood came over her and made her commit such a grisly murder, but that wasn't enough to stop them hanging her. Thomas must have been tainted with the same criminal trait.

William Hiron died of his injuries on the Tuesday and the executors of his will posted a reward of 200 guineas for the conviction of the murderers. John Ashfield tracked down Thomas Heytrey at Mr Bradley's farm on Thursday morning and immediately charged him with the murder. Thomas denied it of course, but John pushed him for an explanation of where he was on the Saturday night. Thomas became flustered and couldn't say where he was in any detail. John knew he was on the right track. Thomas couldn't even explain when he had first heard about the incident. John Ashfield sent for Mr Greenway, one of William's executors, to come over to the farm and that afternoon they set about interrogating him in earnest.

In the farm parlour Mr Greenway laid out the whole reward money in cash on the table and suggested that if Thomas revealed who else was in the plot he may well get the money, and possibly even a free pardon too. The matter was deeply serious for Thomas. If he was found guilty of the crime he would certainly go to the gallows, and he knew exactly what that meant after watching his sister hang. The prospect of a free pardon was too good an opportunity to miss. He promptly confessed that it was all the idea of Samuel Sidney, Henry Adams and Nathaniel Quiney. He only suggested the victim and had taken no part in the actual attack. Trying to weasel his way out of

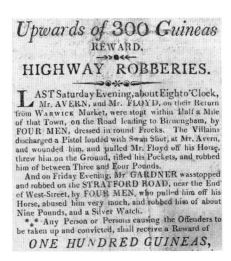

Above left: The *Warwickshire Advertiser* carried desperate appeals to stop the highwaymen.

Above right: Almost invisible from the road, Littleham Bridge was the scene of a violent ambush.

trouble, he said that he had hidden behind the bridge because he would have been too easy to identify. He wasn't really guilty at all. John Ashfield didn't believe a word of it, and neither did Mr Greenway. The reward money went back into Mr Greenway's pocket and John Ashfield sent word to the town's other constable to round up Sidney, Adams and Quiney.

Once all four highway robbers were in custody, it fell to John Ashfield to try and find some evidence to confirm Thomas Heytrey's confession. He went around to his lodgings at Mrs Mercer's house at Pimlico and searched it thoroughly. Mrs Mercer told him that Thomas had not got back to the house on Saturday night until well after nine o'clock. John had already worked out that the robbery had taken place earlier than that. William had left Warwick on his horse on Saturday afternoon after voting in the Parliamentary elections. A search of Thomas's room found a wooden box with several £1 notes in it. Not only was this deeply suspicious for a supposedly penniless jobbing blacksmith, but at least one of the notes appeared to be one of the ones stolen from William Hiron. In those days £1 notes were the property of each private bank rather than the Bank of England and were much easier to trace. It was pretty damning evidence.

The town's lock-up was far too small to properly question all four suspects. Since John Ashfield lived at the Falcon Inn, it was decided to question them there. The four were first given as much ale as they cared to drink, which seems to have been plenty, and then individually interrogated, again with the reward money and possible promise of pardon held out as an incentive. It wasn't long before Mr Greenway and William's brother Henry had four signed confessions. Once again the reward money was then withdrawn and no one could remember saying anything about a free pardon. The four were promptly sent to Warwick to be tried for murder.

At their trial on 10 April, Thomas Heytrey, Henry Adams, Nathaniel Quiney and Samuel Sidney all protested that the confessions had been extracted by getting them drunk first, but the judge wasn't in the slightest bit sympathetic. He sentenced them all to the gallows. He simply wasn't interested in Thomas's defence that he had taken no part in the assault, he was in the plot and that made him as guilty as the rest of them. They were hanged outside Warwick Gaol two days later. Thomas may well have been the ringleader of the gang; it was him who decided that they would set the ambush at Littleham Bridge, although the plot was originally to waylay the bailiff from a nearby farm who would have been returning from market with lots of cash. It was bad luck for William Hiron that the fog was so thick that they mistook him for the bailiff. Samuel Sidney was already renowned for being a vicious brute of a man; he carried a 'walking stick' that could be transformed into a mallet by turning the head around. Quiney and Adams both stated that it was Sidney who went back to William Hiron as he lay stunned in the road and beat him about the head with this mallet. According to Adams, the sound was like that of him hitting his boots with a stick.

Above left: John Ashfield was brought up in his father's inn, the Falcon.

Above right: The villains were publicly hung in front of Warwick Gaol.

The case was startling and unusual. Most of the crime that John Ashfield had to deal with was far more mundane, but also revealed the stark inequalities of society. By 1824, John Ashfield was a respected member of the town's social order. He had taken over the lease of the Falcon from his father and was earning a substantial income from that as well as acting as constable. He was also appointed Overseer of the Poor for the Old Town parish. In those days, before the introduction of the infamous Union Workhouse, most paupers were looked after at home. There was a small workhouse in Henley Street, and the almshouses in Church Street, but most elderly or destitute people were looked after at home with money raised by the Poor Rate. John Ashfield had to administer this.

Of the many cases brought by John Ashfield to the Borough Court, several show the harsh nature of this social welfare. In 1828 he had to prosecute Sarah Munford for returning to Stratford from Alveston. She had already been deported back to her village once and being a pauper, she had to remain in her home parish. Not only did he have to impose this somewhat Draconian law, but he also had to chase up the people who didn't pay their Poor Rate. The wealthier the farmer, the less they felt like paying to feed the poor of the parish and John Ashfield had to bring them to court to force them to pay. Mind you, he forgot to pay his own rates in 1839 and was prosecuted by the other constable. Another element of social welfare that he had to police were the maintenance payments for illegitimate children. Although the paupers of the parish weren't allowed to travel, salesmen moved around just as much then as now. George Guest, a button maker from Bromsgrove, visited Stratford fairly regularly and whilst he was here managed to get Ann Sumner pregnant. John Ashfield had to ensure that he paid maintenance for the child. It was by no means an isolated case; just months later a shoemaker from Naunton in Worcestershire was also prosecuted for not paying for his productive dalliance with another Stratford girl, Elizabeth Hancox. Three days after that Thomas Parker was up in court for arrears of maintenance for the child of Elizabeth Bury. Presumably there was something in the air in 1827.

Being the constable of a small town had its drawbacks. John Ashfield originally ran across Charles Houghton in 1829 and prosecuted him for running his boat on the Lord's Day. It was a fairly trivial offence but it seems that Charles never forgot it, for years later in 1852 we read of Charles, now a wealthy coal dealer, assaulting John as he went about his duties.

The 1820s were turbulent times. On several occasions the town erupted into violence, and there was a constant trickle of cases of theft of food. On the farms around the town cases of arson were not unknown, hay ricks were set on fire and the countryside was awash with the discontent that was to erupt in the Swing Riots. At the start of May 1828 the hay ricks in the farm yard on the Alcester Road were deliberately fired. John Ashfield could find no clue as to who set them ablaze, despite the farmer being sent a letter foretelling the disaster. A week later his policing skills as a thief taker were put to the test in earnest.

At the end of business on Saturday 9 May, the apprentice William Salmon put up the shutters of Thomas Gibbs' shop in High Street. They were heavy solid things, designed to keep the jewellery and watches in the shop safe. Thomas Gibbs was a watchmaker by trade and kept hundreds of pounds worth of clocks, watches, silver and gold plate, rings and brooches. The small and valuable stock was kept in a glass cabinet on the counter and the shop connected directly to the parlour of the house. Thomas checked everything was secure before he went to bed at eleven that night, and slept soundly until the next morning.

In the dead of the night, four men stealthily approached the house and proceeded to lever out the bars holding one of the shutters closed. With the shutter loose they then broke the glass of the parlour window and one of them quickly entered the shop through the parlour. In a matter of moments the entire contents of the glass cabinet was inside a sack and the men made their getaway. Thomas Gibbs slept through it all.

Modernised in the late nineteenth century, the Plume of Feathers is still going strong.

The four men were heard leaving Stratford by the Birmingham Road, although they weren't immediately connected with the burglary. At first light Thomas Gibbs came downstairs and realised what had happened. He immediately raised the alarm, sending for John Ashfield and also his friend Thomas Lowe, a farmer from Binton. John Ashfield was first on the scene and soon discovered that the gang had been heard leaving the town in the early hours heading towards Birmingham. Thomas Lowe arrived, bringing with him some horses to help in the pursuit. The two of them set off after the rogues.

They stopped every now and then to see if anyone had any more information. It seems that there was enough to encourage them on all the way to Shirley, where they stopped at the Plume of Feathers pub. John and Thomas stepped into the pub, little suspecting their reception.

There, sat on the floor, were the four robbers, their hats in front of them, sharing out the loot. In a second William Slatter jumped and pulled out a pistol. John froze for a heart-stopping second as the flint lock clicked and hissed, and breathed again as the gun misfired. John jumped for Slatter and another man, grabbing both of them, one in each hand. Thomas Lowe went after William Vale, who dived out of the door. Thomas raced after him, leaving John Ashfield hanging on to two furious villains who promptly started kicking and punching the living daylights out of him. He had to let go of them both and they fled out of the door but the fourth man, John Windsor, ran into the parlour and tried to jump through the window. John Ashfield chased after him. Windsor bounced off the window casement and then ran down into the cellar. John followed him and after a considerable fight managed to restrain him.

Catherine Richards, the landlady, watched helplessly as her pub was smashed up in the brief but vicious fight. With John Windsor trussed up, Thomas Lowe returned dragging an exhausted William Vale. He had chased him across two fields and finally cornered him in a hovel where he was trying to hide a tortoiseshell comb in a pile of manure. The two of them then set off to see who else they could find. William Slatter was soon found hiding in a holly bush across the fields, but of the other man there was no trace.

With the three villains secured, John Ashfield made a thorough search and found that almost all of the jewellery was either stashed in the hats on the floor, one of which had John Windsor's name written inside, or in the pockets of the men. John Windsor also had a black leather pocketbook in which he had been making a list of all the items as they were shared out amongst the gang. It was quite a haul. Slatter had a gold brooch, a roll of coral and a silver scent box in his pockets, Vale had some combs and the rest of the pieces still in the hats on the floor ranged from silver watches and sugar tongs to gold seals, rings, bracelets and ear rings. This was, of course, a Stratford robbery, and so there was even a cross carved from the mulberry tree that Shakespeare planted. Looking around the pub, John Ashfield discovered a 'dark lanthorn' hanging behind the cellar door; it was a shuttered lantern used by rogues who wanted to show as little light as possible.

Old flintlock pistols were liable to misfire, luckily for John Ashfield.

The three robbers were quickly sent to Warwick Gaol and their trial was set for the Midsummer Assizes. By July the fourth man still had not been caught, and Slatter, Vale and Windsor never divulged his name, despite some intense questioning. The judge was not impressed by this uncooperative attitude, and even less impressed by Slatter's insistence that he 'was as innocent as a newborn child', particularly in view of the way he had tried to shoot John Ashfield. All three men were found guilty and sentenced to death.

John Ashfield was the hero of the town. Over the years he had given sterling service and everyone thought it was high time he received some sort of formal thanks. There was a public subscription held and at a town meeting on 21 July he was presented with a massive silver cup, weighing 44oz, engraved with the following:

> This cup was presented on 21 July 1828 to John Ashfield, Constable of Stratford upon Avon, by the inhabitants of that town and neighbourhood to evince their approbation of his conduct in the execution of his office.

It was also engraved with a picture of a falcon with its wings outstretched.

A few weeks later Slatter, Vale and Windsor had their death sentences commuted to transportation for life and were sent to the hulk *Retribution* to await their journey to the penal colony in Australia. John Ashfield returned to his duties as constable as one of the most respected men in the town.

John Ashfield had gained an extensive knowledge of the people of Stratford and it gradually gained him an almost legendary status. On 8 December 1831, Richard Phillips decided to steal a mare and gelding from his master, John Cross. Once Mr Cross had left the house in the morning he got the groom to saddle the mare and put a bridle onto the gelding so that he could exercise them. In fact, he trotted off towards Birmingham and later that afternoon was trying to sell them to Noah Parrott, a rather dodgy used horse dealer in Aston. Mr Cross alerted John Ashfield and the following morning he set off in pursuit of Phillips, judging quite correctly that he would fail to sell the horses in Birmingham and make for Leicester afterwards. He arrested Phillips there that afternoon. Mr Cross was at a loss to explain Phillips' uncharacteristic behaviour. At the trial he told the judge that the man had been the best servant he had ever had and must have been insane to steal the horses. Despite this glowing endorsement the judge sentenced Phillips to death.

The election of 1832 was the first of a series that were to introduce reform to English politics. The Reform Act was really designed to give the new middle classes a say in running things. The poor old workers didn't get a look in as usual. The Act itself was repeatedly blocked in the House of Lords by the aristocracy who were quite happy with the status quo. By the time of the election in December everyone had worked themselves into a right tiz. Riots were breaking out all over the country; five people were killed in Sheffield. The regiment of the Scots Greys was called out onto the streets of Warwick and in Nuneaton the militia actually performed a cavalry charge into a crowd of protesters, complete with drawn sabres. Dozens were injured and a Mr Glover died under the hooves of the horses. The Coroner of Stratford, Mr Hunt, was called to hold the inquest. To the utter astonishment of everyone present he declared that it was an 'accidental death'.

The election in Stratford was not quite as traumatic. The population of the town was now somewhere around 4,000, but there were only ninety-nine voters. For days before the election there were scuffles in the streets as the impoverished agricultural labourers sought to impress on the Whig and Tory voters the need for reform, the abolition of the Corn Laws and the cruelty of having one's granny dragged off to the workhouse. Tempers were rather stretched on the 17th. As ever, John Ashfield was smack in the middle of it all.

There seem to have been two main mobs. One gathered outside the Cross Keys in Ely Street and made its way across to the White Lion in Henley Street. Once there they started to pelt the windows of the pub with stones until there wasn't a pane left. John Ashfield could do little to prevent the damage on his own. The other constable, John Keeley, had his hands full with another mob growing outside the Shakespeare. Both mobs were in excess of 100 people. All thoughts of political protest had gone out of the window and the bricks were flying in earnest. John Ashfield seems to have given up on the crowd outside the White Lion and gone to the aid of Constable Keeley. He had been kicked and punched for long enough and was making notes of the worst culprits and ringleaders for future reference. In particular he noticed a stranger in the town who seemed to be intent on stirring things up, especially when it came to kicking constables.

The local gentry sent a rider to Coventry to call out the militia. This was all far more than the two town constables could handle. By the time order was restored, John Ashfield had quite a list of fractious locals, but who was the stranger? By chance he walked into the Bricklayers Arms and there he was, complete with a cudgel hidden under his coat. John Ashfield arrested Frederick Lewis for rioting and assaulting him in the execution of his duty. He also arrested another four people, including Thomas Jackson, aged only twelve. John Keeley had a similar list of arrests, seven people ranging in age from eighteen to forty-two. All the rioters were sent off to Warwick Gaol to await their trial. Both constables had been beaten black and blue during the riot.

This photograph of John Ashfield was taken a couple of years before he died. He had become a local legend.

The trial was something of a muted affair. All the men pleaded not guilty at first, but the judges actually paid attention to Mrs Riddler of the White Lion when she pleaded for clemency for them. The men changed their pleas to guilty and were bound over to keep the peace. Frederick Lewis was singled out to explain his actions. He told the court how he had been born in France, and so had no home parish to go to. He had trained to make musical instruments but could find no work since finishing his apprenticeship. He had walked from Bristol to Birmingham, on to Nottingham and was in Stratford on his way to London. He had just about had enough of the unfairness of it all. It was a widely held sentiment.

Not that all of England's problems were solved by this election; it would take another couple of decades to sort out the worst excesses of the old system. However, it was enough to prevent England descending into anarchy and revolution the way that much of Europe did at the time.

John Ashfield's career as a policeman gradually faded as he was promoted to Sheriff's Bailiff and younger men took on the strenuous work of chasing thieves. In 1835, new legislation transformed local government and the town finally got another two constables and a properly constituted police force. John bought the freehold of the Falcon and farmland alongside the Evesham Road. He retired a wealthy and well-respected member of the town and eventually died in July 1873.

CHAPTER THREE

—◆—

CAROLINE EDDEN'S CLOSE SHAVE

'Please God if I live till morning...'

These days Windsor Street has little to recommend it. A car park and a coach park take up most of its length, with just a few historic buildings close to the junction with Greenhill Street. Back in Shakespeare's day the north side was just market gardens, but later these were developed into really low class hovels and courts. By the eighteenth century it was locally called Hell Lane. In 1842 it was called Windsor Street but the warrens of dilapidated houses and courts had reached their peak and it was one of the more dubious parts of town.

Caroline Edden moved into a house in one of the courts off Windsor Street in the summer of 1842. These courts were similar to the famous back-to-backs of the industrial cities, a collection of badly built two-storey houses around a yard with a communal water pump and privy. The houses were so flimsy that Ann Jones, who lived in the next house to Caroline, could hear absolutely everything that went on inside. Indeed, even William Smith, the mason who lived across the court, could hear pretty much everything too. Ann Jones didn't even need to hold a glass to the wall to catch the scandal.

Caroline Edden was in her thirties and a single woman. She also had something of a reputation and was known locally as Pinkie. Ann Jones despaired at the number of times men would call late at night, and presumably keep her awake with their goings on. Caroline had moved to the court to be able to get away from her violent and abusive boyfriend, the Warwick butcher Henry Goddin. She had left after he threatened to cut her head off once too often. As is often the way, he didn't take the hint and tracked her down to her new house.

Henry Goddin turned up out of the blue on Saturday 24 October and asked her out for a drink at the Falstaff pub. He was in a cheerful mood and bought her several gins. In the course of their conversation he offered to give her a bedstead and mattress for her new home, but she turned him down, telling him in no uncertain terms that it was her house and she wanted nothing more from him. He managed to conceal his disappointment and they parted amicably enough later that afternoon.

Previously called Hell Lane, Windsor Street was once home to some dreadful slums.

At about ten o'clock on the Sunday night, Caroline had a meagre supper, a pot of tea and then undressed for bed. Not long after, who should start banging on the door but Henry Goddin. She told him to go away several times, but eventually he leaned hard on the door and burst the flimsy wooden latch open. Ann Jones had heard him banging, but didn't hear the latch breaking. Once inside Henry begged Caroline for some food and she let him polish off what was left on the table and finish the cold tea. He then insisted on getting into bed with her, just for a couple of hours he promised. He was fairly drunk and in no mood to be gainsaid.

'Please God, if I live till morning, I will have this stopped.' she muttered to herself. The two of them drifted off to an uneasy sleep.

At first light the ill-matched pair stirred. Caroline told Henry to get dressed and get out but Henry said he had better wait until the neighbour had finished getting ready. Caroline slipped back off into a warm doze.

Suddenly she felt a searing pain across her throat. Reaching up, her hand closed on the blade of a knife cutting into her neck. Heedless of the pain as the blade sliced through to the bone, she dragged the knife away and leapt from the bed.

'Murder!' she screamed at the top of her voice, blood pouring down across the flimsy shift she was wearing. Henry Goddin stood up and made a slash at his own throat, but the blade was now blunt. He paused to sharpen the blade on his steel and Caroline seized the chance to bolt for the door and the safety of Ann Jones' house.

The whole court was now wide awake. William Smith sent for PC Reason while Ann Jones tried to stop Caroline from bleeding to death. She had a deep ragged cut across her throat, and luckily it hadn't pierced any of the vital arteries, but she was still losing a lot of blood. Timothy and Mary Dickens, who lived further down the court, ran to get the surgeon, David Rice. He turned up at much the same time as PC Reason.

David Rice assessed Caroline to be out of danger once he got there, and left her in the care of his apprentice whilst he and PC Reason went into Caroline's house to see what had happened to Henry Goddin. They found him lying naked on the bed surrounded by a growing pool of blood. He had clearly sharpened the knife quite well enough; there was a gash four inches long and three deep across his throat, severing the windpipe. He was still alive.

The surgeon managed to stitch up the huge open wound in Goddin's neck, but he wasn't at all sure that it would much help. Goddin was transferred to a bed in the dispensary whilst Caroline was taken to the hospital ward in the Union Workhouse. Over the next few days she started to recover from her sudden ordeal. Goddin languished, an apologetic nervous wreck. He told David Rice that he just wanted to die, and couldn't he give him something to polish him off. The surgeon was under instructions to try to keep him alive so that he could be tried for attempted murder.

Little now remains to show what a warren of squalid buildings once housed some of the town's poorest citizens.

A week passed and Henry Goddin died on the next Sunday. An inquest was held on the Monday, with the coroner and jurors going to the workhouse to interview Caroline. She was still weak but managed to give them the main events. Henry Goddin's brother Michael was summoned to cast some insight into Henry's character. He couldn't add much to what was already known. Henry Goddin was a man with a very short temper and a tendency to drink to excess all too frequently. Michael did add one new element; Henry had fallen from a loft when he was about eighteen and suffered serious head injuries. Since that accident, his character had turned increasingly violent. His career as a butcher had possibly hardened an already callous character.

The jury decided that Caroline had suffered an attempted murder by Henry Goddin and that he had then killed himself in remorse. Since this was a case of suicide, the law was that his body had to be buried within a day of the inquest, and that it had to be done between nine o'clock and midnight. An uneasy peace settled on the slum that was Windsor Street.

CHAPTER FOUR

—❖—

THE MURDER OF CONSTABLE WILLIAM TILSLEY

'Damn your eyes! I'll shoot you.'

Christmas usually puts a strain on most families, and the more dysfunctional the family, the bigger the rows after lunch. Nevertheless, no one expected Christmas 1842 at Spernal Farm to end up in such a spectacular tragedy.

The Crowley family was about as dysfunctional as you could imagine. The father, William, ran the farm, whilst his eldest son, Henry, had left home to become a shopkeeper and merchant in Liverpool. Joseph, the second son, remained to help with the farm and the youngest, James, was generally described as 'violent, dissipated, extravagant and of unruly disposition'. He was thirty and blessed with good looks, light brown hair, bright eyes and was 5ft 9ins tall. James also had a lover in Washwood Heath, didn't bother going to church, and was a long way from being suitably respectful to his parents. It probably didn't help matters when he published a pamphlet stating how dreadfully they had treated him, how they didn't give him enough money to live on and a whole litany of other complaints.

People who knew the family thought that this was a bit rich. Old William Crowley had got so fed up with the ceaseless whining, not to mention threats of violence, that he had arranged to pay James £1 a week, the use of a horse and all the costs of keeping it, as long as he took lodgings away from the farmhouse. James moved into the blacksmith's spare room just a scant 300 yards from the farm. It wasn't really far enough away.

James continued to harass his father through the spring of 1842, with increasing use of threats to try and bully more money from the old man. It got to the point where William seriously began to fear for his safety and so he got his labourer, William Tilsley, sworn in as a Special Constable. William was a big lad, just twenty years old, and quite capable of thrashing James in a fight. He lived in the village of Sambourne, not far away, together with his wife and two children. Once he was sworn in as a Special Constable, he had the authority to arrest James if his behaviour became too threatening.

St Leonard's Church was at the heart of the diffuse village of Spernal.

Throughout the summer James continued to carp on about how unfairly he was being treated and pestering his father for extra money to fund his various vices. Everything seemed to be pointing towards some sort of crisis by Christmas. With that in mind, William Crowley sent William Tilsley round to the blacksmith's on 22 December to tell James that he would not be welcome at the farm on Christmas Day, even though all the rest of the family would be gathering there for the festivities. It must have been slightly provocative, but everyone was thoroughly fed up with him and his constant whining. William Tilsley was invited to stay at the farm over the Christmas holiday to provide full-time protection for the family. They really were that frightened of what James might do.

Of course, James just had to turn up and spoil everything. At nine o'clock in the morning on Christmas Day he appeared in the parlour demanding to see his father.

The old man sat in his chair, with William Tilsley standing protectively at his side. James repeated his demands for more money and when that met a distinctly chilly response, he made out that he had a pistol in his pocket and said he would shoot the old man.

'Here I am, shoot away,' the old man called his bluff.

William intervened, 'You had better leave him alone, and you had better be quiet.' William Tilsley escorted the seething James out of the house as he muttered, 'I will see you about this another day, old gentleman.'

James' mother ran off across the fields after him to try and calm him down. It didn't work very well; James told her he would meet the old b****** in the field in three-quarters of an hour. No one went to see if he was there at the due time.

James Crowley arrived at the Horseshoe after riding fifty-six miles in one afternoon.

At about one o'clock, James' mother looked out of the window and saw him walking back across the field, holding a double-barrelled shotgun. She ran to her husband and begged him to go and hide upstairs. He was having none of it, but she dragged him bodily to the foot of the stairs. Just then they heard the sound of a window breaking. He needed no more encouragement.

Outside William Tilsley was patrolling the grounds with another labourer, Joseph Street, and the farm boy, Nicholls. They heard the window break and ran around to the yard to see what was happening. Everyone's nerves were stretched. They found James standing by the window that he had just broken with the butt of the gun. He rounded on them, raising the shotgun.

'What! You're coming are you? Damn your eyes! I'll shoot you.'

James fired the shotgun directly at William Tilsley. The blast caught him in the eye and blew his brains out of the back of his head, all over the yard. He dared the remaining two to come and get him, but they were already fleeing for cover. James turned on his heel and walked back to the blacksmith's cottage.

William Tilsley lay dead in the yard as the old man and the other labourers crept out of hiding. He had died instantly. They put his body in the woodshed and sent out for help and to raise the alarm for the fugitive James Crowley. It was a Christmas Day that nobody in Spernal would ever forget.

Crowley took the mail coach from the George the same evening.

William Tilsley was laid to rest in St Peter's Church at Coughton.

You might be tempted to think that a quick getaway in 1842 was out of the question. James Crowley walked back to his lodgings and packed a bag with all his money; some £200, a small fortune. He saddled up his horse, a bright bay with black legs, some fifteen hands tall, and cantered off. He rode to Stratford first and then on to Coventry. He found no way of getting quickly away from there. It was Christmas Day and there was no mail coach. He then rode back towards Stratford, skirting the town just in case the alarm had reached there and then on to Shipston-on-Stour. He arrived at the Horseshoe Inn at five o'clock. The horse was pretty much dead on its feet after cantering fifty-four miles. He put it into the pub stables and ordered himself a jug of cider. Then he walked about the town, inquiring about buying a pair of spectacles – you know what it's like when you pack in a hurry. He couldn't find a suitable pair. He then went to the George Inn and booked a ticket on the mail coach to Steventon. This connected to the Great Western

Railway and managed to get him there in time to catch the night mail to London. Once in London his trail vanished. It was believed that he then caught a ship to America, but no one ever found out what really happened to him. Many people in Spernal thought that he was so unhinged that he would commit suicide.

In Spernal an inquest was held and James Crowley indicted for the murder of William Tilsley. William himself was then buried in the churchyard at Coughton. He was the first policeman to be killed on duty in Warwickshire, though sadly not the last... as we shall see.

CHAPTER FIVE

—◇—

VICTORIAN CHILD
MURDERS

Inevitably, it was the most vulnerable members of society that bore the brunt of mankind's inhumanity. There are few more vulnerable than children and Stratford, like many a town, has an ignoble past in this respect.

The social values of the era didn't help a great deal. As the Reform Acts altered the way the Poor Laws were administered, they introduced the dismal spectacle of the Union Workhouse, a place so dreaded that many would prefer to die in a ditch than enter its dark and sadistic regime. In John Ashfield's day, the poor were given dole money at home and only taken into institutional care as a last resort. This came to an end with the Poor Law Unions, where groups of villages and towns would combine to build a workhouse and send all their paupers there rather than allow them to stay at home. The result was a new category of crime in the Victorian courts.

If an unmarried girl became pregnant there was intense pressure on her to name the father so that he could be forced to pay maintenance. For poor girls there was the option of having the baby in the workhouse, but it wasn't a popular choice. If nothing else, the mortality rate of babies in these institutions was high, and the living conditions were so degrading that few availed themselves of the option.

Lydia Gardiner and her sister Elizabeth were servants at Pillerton Priors in 1854. Lydia was twenty-three and Elizabeth twenty-nine. Lydia had managed to get herself pregnant and wasn't going to name the father, much to the annoyance of the Poor Law Relief Officer, John Reading. On 5 February he visited Lydia at work and once again tried to get the name of the guilty lad out of her, but she was still not co-operating. It was obvious that the baby was due any day now and so he offered her a ticket to allow her to enter the workhouse and have the baby there. She refused. She would rather take her chances.

The winter of 1855 was wickedly cold. When the wheelwright William Mason walked from the nearby village of Ettington to Whatcote on the morning of 10 February he had to push his way through snowdrifts. As he crossed the main Banbury road he noticed Lydia and Elizabeth walking along it, but gave it no more thought

Pillerton Priors is a small village on the road to Banbury.

and carried on to his work at Whatcote. A couple of hours later he returned the same way and, a couple of hundred yards from the Fullready turn on the high road, he saw a pool of blood in the snow. There was a trail of it leading to a snowdrift. He brushed the snow aside and revealed the body of a baby. Horrified he rushed off to get the local constable, Thomas Mann.

The two of them returned to the scene and William dug out the little corpse and placed it in a linen bag. As he was doing this he noticed Lydia and Elizabeth come along the road, see them and hurry off in the opposite direction. Thomas Mann chased after them and when he caught up with them asked if either of them had been ill. Both denied any such thing and insisted on heading back to Pillerton. The constable had no reason to suspect anything at that point and let them go on. Back at the grisly snowdrift, William Mason had discovered a second trail of blood leading off down the road. The two of them followed it to the cottage of Miss Ann Hitchman.

Miss Hitchman told them of how the two girls had turned up on her doorstep, soaking wet and half frozen. She had brought them inside and settled them down in front of the fire, giving them mugs of warm beer to thaw them out. The two girls asked her if there was any chance of getting a cart to take them to Wellesbourne, but with the roads blocked with snow it was a forlorn hope. Revived, the two girls thanked her and left.

Thomas Mann examined the chair by the fire and was alarmed to see spots of blood on the floor and cushion. It all needed further investigation. He took the body of the baby to the pub in Ettington. Here the landlady of the Nelson was instructed to guard the little corpse until the surgeon could get there. Constable Mann sent word to Wellesbourne to get the surgeon, Mr Richard Pitt, to conduct an autopsy. He then went to find Lydia and Elizabeth.

Lydia Gardiner was charged with wilful murder that afternoon. She denied that the baby had ever moved and so was a stillbirth. The way the law stood in those days, if a child breathed, then it was considered to be alive and capable of being murdered, if it didn't breath then it had no independent life and thus could not be murdered. However its birth had to be notified to the authorities in either case. When John Reading came to visit Lydia on 13 February he said he was very sorry to see the state she was in and pointedly said he hoped she had not laid violent hands on the child. She assured him that the baby had never moved.

The surgeon Richard Pitt was coming to a very different conclusion as he performed the autopsy. The lungs of the child were fully inflated, proving that it had drawn breath. It was a bit academic, since the poor mite had promptly died from the intense cold. Being born on the side of a road in midwinter was hardly conducive to a long life. Although initially charged with wilful murder, Lydia was subsequently brought to trial at Warwick Assizes on a charge of concealing a birth. Elizabeth was charged with aiding and abetting her. The surgeon's evidence was put to one side after the circumstances of the birth were considered. They were found guilty; Lydia was sentenced to four months' hard labour and her sister two months.

Lydia gave birth to her child in a snowdrift here.

Lydia Gardiner's story is by no means unique. The workhouse held such terrors that many girls tried to conceal the birth of an illegitimate child rather than submit to its ghastly regime. This was a world with no contraception, where abortion was illegal and the stigma of a bastard baby would ruin the life of a young woman. It comes as no surprise that in 1858, no less than three infants were found drowned in the Stratford Canal. Their mothers were never identified.

In small villages the locals tried to keep things quiet. In 1856 Jane Smith, the servant at George Court's farm in Charlecote, had a baby late on the night of Sunday 30 March. She quietly strangled the child and wrapped it up in an old apron, placing it on a chair in her bedroom and covering that with a dress. She presumably hoped that she would be able to dispose of the body later on. On 1 April, Esther Court noticed some blood stains on the floor and discovered the dubious looking parcel. Esther called Jane's mother, Zilphah Smith, to come and talk to her daughter. They called the surgeon, Henry Rollason, from Wellesbourne, who certified the baby was dead, but he was not at all happy about the way it had died. They told him it was a stillbirth and that matters should be left at that. The other farmers of the village closed ranks and put pressure on him to let the matter drop. It was three weeks before Henry managed to pressure the Stratford police into pressing charges of wilful murder against Jane. The case still foundered, with the minor charge of concealment of birth being taken forward rather than murder.

Jane Smith strangled her child in the village of Charlecote.

Was the body discovered at Drybank Farm that of Rees Brandish?

Not two miles from that bloodstained snowdrift stands Drybank Farm. It was here on 13 November 1897 that the police dug up the badly corroded body of a little boy. The corpse had been buried in the cabbage patch in a pit of quicklime. There wasn't enough left for them to clearly identify the child with the primitive forensic techniques of the day. They certainly had their suspicions though.

A couple of months previously the farmer's sister, Elizabeth Brandish, had collected her illegitimate son, Rees Brandish, from the care of Sarah Urben in Ashford, Kent. Sarah had been paid weekly to look after the child so that Elizabeth could continue her career as a nurse. Elizabeth had kept the child's existence a close secret, especially from her new boyfriend. He was a policeman in Clent and couldn't tarnish his respectable reputation by consorting with a woman with a bastard child. Elizabeth couldn't hide the weekly payments from him forever, so decided to do something about it.

Apparently Elizabeth met a woman whilst out walking on the Clent hills who said that she was childless and would dearly love to have a little boy. Rees was now two years old, and incurably cute according to the letters Elizabeth received from Sarah Urben. If this woman was to adopt Rees, all Elizabeth's problems would be solved. She could marry Sergeant Narramore and live happily ever after. According to Elizabeth they agreed to the adoption.

The autopsy at the Chequers Inn failed to identify the corpse of the child.

Elizabeth collected her son from Ashford on 10 September and started the long journey back to Ettington. The following day they boarded a train from Towcester to Ettington. It was a slow train, stopping at every country station. Elizabeth upgraded her ticket from the open second class carriage to a first class compartment. It wasn't a corridor carriage so once the train was moving they were alone. The guard saw the little boy when he checked the train at Kineton Station, but when the train stopped at Ettington apparently only Elizabeth got off. She was carrying a tin trunk. That brief glimpse of Rees by the guard at Kineton was the last anyone saw of the boy.

The trunk was carried by cart to the farm and Elizabeth made no mention of the boy whilst she stayed with her relatives. After a few days she went back to her work at Clent, although she visited the farm once again a week later. In the meantime, Sarah Urben was becoming concerned over the fate of the child she had so carefully nurtured. First she contacted the vicar at Ettington, but received no adequate explanation of what had happened to Rees. She then contacted the police.

The police investigated, decided something was definitely amiss and arrested Elizabeth. She told them that she had met the childless woman once again on the train and left Rees with her. Unfortunately she had not found out her name or address.

The investigating officer was not convinced and ordered a detailed search of the farm. It was then that the lime-filled grave was discovered, containing the body of a child approximately the same age and weight as Rees. The body had the same number of teeth and the same colour hair as well. Beyond this there was no definitive evidence that the body was that of the missing child.

Elizabeth Brandish was tried twice for the murder of her child. In both trials the lack of identification of the body was to prove an insuperable obstacle to her conviction. The police simply could not prove that the body was that of Rees and without that proof, Elizabeth could possibly have been telling the truth when she said that she gave the child to a stranger. It seemed highly suspicious, but even in Victorian times you couldn't send someone to the gallows on a vague suspicion.

For some, childhood never really ended. Alice Ashfield grew up in her family home in Illmington. She was deaf and dumb, handicapped from birth and, vulnerable as she was, relied on the support of her mother and sisters. They understood her gestures and grunts but she could never enjoy a normal social life. She was twenty-two in 1853.

On 1 October 1853 she was walking in the village when she was spotted by a couple of very nasty characters, William Keeley and William Woodward. They saw that she had stumbled in the street and offered to take the trusting girl home, leading her by the hand across the empty fields between Illmington and Darlingscot. Once out of the sight of the village they stripped and repeatedly raped her. They thought that since she was both deaf and dumb, there was no way that she could identify them.

The picturesque village of Illmington was the scene of a dreadful assault on Alice Ashfield.

Some hours later Alice managed to struggle home, having been left battered and bleeding by the two rogues. Over the next few days she managed to communicate her dreadful ordeal to her sister by signs. The village was horrified to discover that two apparently upright citizens had descended to such barbarism and the police were called. Much to their own surprise, Keeley and Woodward were arrested and sent to Warwick Gaol. At the 1854 Lent Assizes, Alice gave evidence, interpreted by her sister. The two men were sentenced to twenty years transportation, with hard labour.

CHAPTER SIX

—◆—

THE OUTHILL FARM OUTRAGE

'Well, if I can't have her...'

Outhill Farm is one of many on the edge of Stratford district. It lies to the north-east, between Henley and Studley, and the area was comparatively sparsely populated in 1861. Like all farms of that period, it comprised of the farmer and his family, together with domestic servants and labourers living in the house as well. Outhill Farm was unusual in that Mr Davis Edge, the farmer, was a young single man. His aunt, Ann Mills Davis, lived with him and had the role of housekeeper. The only domestic servant was Sarah Kirby, a pretty girl, twenty-four years old, and very pious. She had been brought up in the nearby village of Trentham and was a regular attendant at the local Sunday school.

Two of the farm labourers also lived in the farmhouse, William Snape and George Gardner. They were assisted in their work by several other farmhands from the cottages close by. George Gardner had only started work for Mr Edge in the summer of 1861. He was twenty-one, short and stocky and with a sandy coloured set of whiskers and moustache. Most people thought he was a fair bit older than he claimed. It was generally thought that he had a coarse countenance and wasn't the brightest button in the box. As was usual in those days, all the servants had rooms in the top of the farmhouse. Downstairs were a sitting room, parlour, and a front and back kitchen around a main hall.

The autumn saw the start of the trouble. George took a fancy to Sarah, and Sarah was having none of it. George, however, persisted. He teased and pestered her. It seems that he even drilled a hole in the wall of her bedroom so that he could spy on her as she undressed at night. His bedroom was just across the corridor from hers, next door to William Snape's. William wasn't impressed by this, but mostly because he was too short to be able to see through it easily. As autumn passed into winter the atmosphere at the farm soured rapidly. Sarah didn't know about the hole in the wall, but she couldn't help but be annoyed by the constant innuendo and attention George paid to her. He was taking liberties.

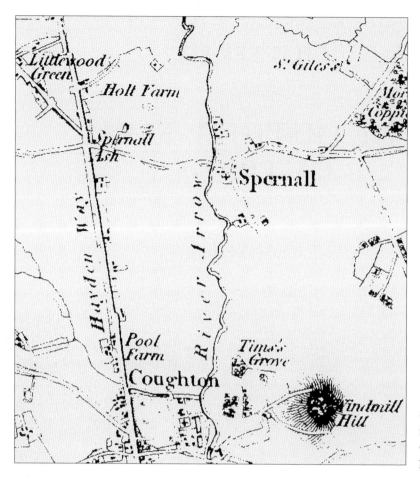

Outhill Farm is on the edge of Spernal parish.

Matters came to a head over Christmas. Sarah told Ann Davis that she was fed up with George's behaviour. She was supposed to be a domestic servant and not the object of constant leering and jibes. Ann Davis understood her problem and talked the matter over with her nephew. It was all a bit delicate, as Mr Edge needed George since he was an experienced waggoner and ploughman, and he needed Sarah Kirby to do all the domestic chores. It wasn't easy to get new staff, except during the autumn hiring fairs in the local towns. Mr Edge took George to one side and told him to mend his ways. George started to argue,

'Well, if I can't have her, then no one shall.' Mr Edge told him not to be so stupid, and George calmed down, promised to behave and stop his unwelcome attentions to the girl. Deep inside, he was seething with fury that she had betrayed him to the master. His feelings of love were turning to hate for the unsuspecting girl. Mr Edge reinforced his advice with the threat of dismissal and there he thought that the matter ended. If only it had.

As spring broke across the land, George was getting into a filthy temper more and more frequently. The young lad that helped him with the horses was on the receiving end of it every now and then. George thrashed him for the most trivial of reasons. Charles Russell was only a teenager and had no way of retaliating. He complained but it did little good; he took to keeping out of George's way as much as he could. George was also drinking far more than was good for him. It was usual for every farm to brew its own beer and every labourer was given a daily allowance. The brewing and dispensing of the beer was Sarah's responsibility and it wasn't long before George was constantly complaining that she wasn't giving him his due amount. Ann Davis was certain that Sarah was behaving entirely fairly with him, but George kept pestering for more. He took to going out to the pub at nights as well. Mr Edge ran the farm along fairly strict lines and locked the doors at ten o'clock each night. There were an increasing number of times when George hadn't come back by then and ended up being locked out. Mr Edge told him that he must improve his ways.

George Gardner fled to Poole's Wood after his deadly attack.

George told another labourer, George Salt, how he wished Sarah was stiff. He would murder and bury her under the turf. Matters weren't improved a few weeks later when George told William Bradley he wanted to 'blow her f***ing brains out'. When William asked why on earth he should want to do that, when she wanted nothing to do with him, George growled that he should never have anything to do with her. William reckoned George was sweet on her, and very jealous.

By April the household was simmering. Out in the fields one day, George was talking with Richard Greenhall. As usual he was muttering about Sarah not giving him enough beer. Richard mentioned that he was spending too many nights out and that he had heard that one more time would see him sacked on the spot. George was furious; it wasn't fair, that Sarah had got it in for him, what had he ever done but ask for his due amount? Richard shut up; there was no reasoning with the man.

George went off to the pub with George Salt that evening. They stayed at the Greyhound until two in the morning. Somewhat the worse for wear, but by no means drunk, they walked back to George Salt's cottage not far from the farm, and George Gardner slept on the floor, unsure of what his reception would be back at Outhill Farm.

Dawn broke on Wednesday 23 April 1862. George Gardner decided he would get straight to work as though nothing was amiss. He was out in the fields at six o'clock, but in a foul mood. Mr Edge set off to Tanworth Fair not long after and noticed George looking a bit wild and dishevelled. Charles Russell managed to make a mess of the horse's harness and George really flew off the handle at him, even threatening to stab him. George asked Charles where Mr Edge was going and was told that he was on his way to Tanworth Fair.

Richard Greenhall stopped by at about eight o'clock as they were taking a break. He noticed George was in a strange mood.

'Is your hat drunk then?' he joked.

'I don't know whether the bitch will draw me any beer. The bitch wants killing.' He went on, 'I wish I had something in my hand and someone before me.'

'Do you mean me?' asked Richard, rather concerned at the way the conversation was turning. The two of them went down to the farmhouse and Sarah duly gave both of them their flagons of beer. They walked back to the fields but Richard had had enough of George's bickering. He left George to his black mood.

George sat alone in the field idly tossing a part of the plough, the share, in his hand, his thoughts darkening by the moment. What would happen when Mr Edge returned from the fair? Why would that blasted girl not give him enough beer? Why should she not love him? Should he kill her like he said?

He tossed the ploughshare up in the air; if it came down on its side, he would walk away. If it fell point first into the ground, then he would kill her.

It landed point first.

It was ten o'clock when he walked into the back kitchen and demanded more beer. Sarah stood up from the washing and told him he had had his quota. They stood for a while in the silent kitchen and he then asked her to go and fetch the shotgun from the parlour.

Entirely unsuspecting, Sarah crossed the hall into the parlour and picked up the double-barrelled shotgun. Mr Edge normally kept it there, loaded but with the hammers down. He thought it was perfectly safe. Ann Davis saw Sarah carrying it towards the back kitchen and came to see what was going on. Sarah handed the gun to George as Ann walked into the room.

'What are you going to do with that?' George muttered something about rooks, which was normal enough. 'Remember that it is loaded, George.' she added.

'Yes ma'am, I know it is.' he replied.

George pulled back the hammers, removed the two percussion caps, and spiked the tiny holes underneath. It was a common enough action to make sure the gun would fire reliably. He put the caps back. Ann Davis returned to the front kitchen and Sarah turned back to the sink full of washing.

George aimed the shotgun at the back of Sarah's head and fired. She died instantly. The charge of number six shot blew through her neck and into her brain. She toppled backwards to the floor.

Miss Davis heard the shot. She ran back to the kitchen and saw George standing there. There was smoke curling up from the shotgun as he stared at the ruined body of the maid.

'Get out, get out!' yelled Ann.

He turned around, bringing the gun back up to his shoulder. Ann stared down the barrels, fully aware that one of them was still loaded. She span and ran for the parlour, George running only feet behind her. She slammed the door and turned the key just as George hammered into it.

'Open the door!' he shouted. Not surprisingly, she didn't. She heard him go back to the kitchen, and then run back, battering at the door with his shoulder. It was a stout door and he couldn't break it down. She heard him walk back down the hall.

With her heart beating wildly, Ann Davis looked for a way out. The parlour was on the corner of the house, with two windows. As she looked out she saw that George was walking around the building, and he pointed the gun at her once again. She cringed back into the corner of the room where she couldn't be seen, or shot, from either of the windows. George walked further round the house.

Outside, James Dyer was weeding in the garden when he saw George come around the corner. James was another one of the young lads who worked on the farm. He had heard the shot, but thought it was just someone shooting birds. George raised the shotgun and pointed it straight at him. James thought he was just joking and laughed. Perhaps it was this that saved his life; George lowered the gun and went back into the house.

In the parlour Ann Davis heard George come back in. With every footstep in the empty house ringing out loud, she heard him go into the front kitchen, then back into the back one, and once again back into the front one. George started to smash open the locked bureau with a coal hammer. In it was more powder and shot as well as the farm's supply of petty cash. Reckoning that it would take him a fair while to get into the sturdy bureau, she slid up the window and quickly scrambled out into the garden. She sprinted across to the hedge, but it was too high for her to climb. James Dyer watched her in stunned amazement. Quickly she told him what had happened. They got the bucket from the well, which was just big enough for her to use as a step to vault the hedge. James followed her.

Ann sprinted as fast as her skirts would allow across the fields. She came to Martha Holloway's cottage and told her the grisly news, then ran on to the next farm. Mr Savage let her in and quickly locked the doors. He then armed himself and set out to see what was to be done. Martha was hurrying back to Outhill Farm to see what had really happened.

Both Martha and Mark Savage saw George Gardner heading across the fields towards Poole's Wood, still carrying the shotgun. They found Sarah lying on her back in the kitchen. Martha checked her pulse, but she was stone dead. James Dyer came in too, and was shocked to see the gradually growing pool of blood spreading across the kitchen floor. Mr Edge arrived back from Tanworth and was no less horrified. He sent for the local constable and a surgeon then got straight back on his horse and rode hell for leather to Redditch to raise the alarm there. Everyone was terrified that George was hiding in the wood, waiting to murder the rest of them.

In an hour or so, PC Olliver arrived from Tanworth, and set off in pursuit of George. Finding no sign of him in Poole's Wood, he stopped some people walking on the road and learnt that George had been seen walking towards Wootton Wawen with the gun under his arm. He sent word to Alcester Police Station and followed the trail. At Wootton he discovered that George had been seen again, now heading towards Stratford.

By late afternoon George had reached Stratford and disappeared. A very footsore PC Olliver met up with Superintendent Dunbar from Alcester and they started searching the town. The town's police joined in the manhunt, trawling through the pubs and shops. They first discovered that a man answering George's description had been into Cooper's gun shop in New Street and sold him the shotgun for a sovereign. It was a pitifully low and rather suspicious price. At least now they knew that they were chasing an unarmed fugitive. Hunting around the pubs of the area they soon discovered that he had been in one of the pubs and sold the powder flask and shot to a man there. He had been drinking heavily. Eventually someone suggested that they might have heard him talking about going to get a train.

In 1862 Stratford had three railways. There was one on the Birmingham Road for the Stratford Railway going to Hatton, one at the end of New Street going towards Honeybourne and then London and one rather dilapidated wreck of a tramway going to Moreton-in-Marsh. PC Olliver took a gamble and went straight to the closest one, at the end of New Street. He was in luck. The stationmaster recognised their description and told them George had got on the train to Honeybourne; it was just steaming out of sight past the racecourse.

Superintendent Dunbar commandeered one of the stations pony traps and the two of them set off through the gathering dusk at a gallop, trying to overtake the steam train before it reached the connection with the London train at Honeybourne station. Whipping the horse to a frenzy, they lurched along the battered country roads in virtual pitch darkness. Could a horse-drawn trap outrun the very latest steam locomotives? The railway took a straight route whilst the country lanes wandered through every village and hamlet. They grimly battled on through the night.

Their luck held out. At Honeybourne station the train from London had yet to arrive, and George Gardner was sitting on the platform, pretty much blind drunk. They approached him, half expecting a ferocious struggle, but he was too soused to resist. 'I suppose I must go with you,' was all he said when they arrested him.

George Gardner was transferred to Warwick Gaol to await his trial. In the meantime, rumours abounded throughout the Midlands: apparently he came from a bad family in Banbury, his father had killed his mother, three of his brothers had been transported to Australia for manslaughter, and he was going to take the train to London and flee the country. In fact George had not been raised in Banbury at all, but in a village in Worcestershire, ironically called Slaughter. His father was an unassuming labourer who had spent all his working life in one job and there was only one sister who had married and was living a perfectly normal life. George was unaware of all the gossip and spent the time in gaol

HORRIBLE MURDER AT OUTHILL FARM, NEAR STUDLEY.

On Wednesday forenoon an atrocious murder was committed at Outhill Farm, which is about two miles from Studley, four miles from Henley-in-Arden, and five miles from Redditch. For some time past the farm has been occupied by Mr. Edge, a gentleman who is unmarried, and whose aunt, Miss Davis, lives with him as housekeeper. The murderer is a man named George Gardner, who gives his age as, 21, but who appears much older. He is a short, thick-set fellow, with "sandy" whiskers and moustaches, and a sensual cast of countenance. For the last eleven months he has been in the employment of Mr. Edge, as waggoner, and has lived in the house during the whole of that time. His victim is a young woman who had for the last nine months been in the service of Mr. Edge, as domestic servant, and whose name is Sarah Kirby. She was about 24 years old, was a rather good looking girl, and bore the best character; indeed, her master had the utmost confidence in her. She was decidedly pious, and regularly attended a class-meeting held at Studley. During last summer Gardner began to pay his address to the girl, but she repelled him, and when his attentions became so marked as to cause her annoyance, she complained to Mr. Edge on the subject; on this Mr. Edge remonstrated with the man, and told him that if Kirby had any more cause to complain he would at once discharge him. Afterwards Gardner was more reserved, but it would seem that his love for the girl was changed to hatred.

EXECUTION OF GEORGE GARDNER, FOR THE MURDER AT OUTHILL FARM.

On Monday morning George Gardner, the murderer of Sarah Kirby, was hanged in front of the Warwick County Gaol—a fate which he richly merited. Gardner was not a Warwickshire man, but came from the parish of Slaughter, in Worcestershire, where his father, an old man of sixty-three, still lives. He had a stout, firmly-knit frame, with a heavy, unintellectual head, and a countenance anything but prepossessing.

About twelve months ago, Gardner went into the service of Mr. Davis Edge, a farmer, at Outhill, in the parish of Studley, in this county. The farm-house is an isolated one, situated on the brow of a hill which overlooks Redditch, and the surrounding district of Worcestershire, from which it is only separated by a single field. The house is several miles distant from the nearest town, being nearly half way between Henley-in-Arden and Redditch. His victim Sarah Kirby was a learning to read and write. He started to read the Bible, and the prison chaplain expressed a small hope that he may yet come to repentance, salvation and forgiveness.

The case came to court on 11 August. The galleries at Warwick were packed with ghoulish spectators hoping to hear the salacious details. These were in short supply since Sarah had been chaste and virtuous. The story of the spy-hole in the wall went down well though. At the very start the judge asked George if he had a defence counsel, but of course an ordinary farm worker couldn't afford one, so Mr Stephens was appointed by the court to represent him. The evidence was pretty damning, not to mention the weeks of character assassination that had gone on in the local newspapers. Mr Stephens tried to make out that since no one actually saw the gun fired except George Gardner himself, perhaps it had all been a horrible accident and he had pointed the gun at Sarah as a joke, but it had accidentally fired. Nobody could be sure that it was really a murder. It turned out that not even George was falling for this story. He was pretty resigned to his fate by now and watched the proceedings with a visible sense of detachment. Far from nobody believing it was really murder, the entire jury thought it was, and they didn't even bother to retire to consider their verdict. It was guilty.

Lord Chief Baron Pollock summed up the case as a lesson in jealousy, anger and drunkenness. He donned his black cap and pronounced the dreaded words of the death sentence. He gave George a fortnight to reconcile his soul to the Almighty.

Warwick was packed on 26 August. Well over 1,200 people crammed into the street outside the gaol. The windows of the houses opposite thronged with people who had paid good money to get a grandstand view of the hanging. George had been visited by his sister and brother-in-law a couple of times and on the second visit had made a full confession of the murder. Chillingly, he added in his statement, 'I should have killed Miss Davis if I had got near enough to her.' He wrote a farewell statement in a book. It was rather a maudlin prayer hoping for forgiveness and a place in Heaven. Despite everything, his father had not been able to raise the train fare and never managed to visit his son before the dreadful day.

At 10.20 a.m. a couple of warders emerged from the gates of the gaol helping Gardner mount the steps of the scaffold. His legs had been manacled so he had trouble getting up the steps. He walked across to the noose and Mr Smith, the hangman, put it over his neck. Smith then walked over to the bolt, but one of the warders reminded him that he should put a hood over the condemned man's head. Mr Smith fumbled through his pockets trying to find the hood amid a cacophony of cat-calls and jeers. Finally he found it and put it to its intended purpose. He then shook hands with George, walked across to the bolt and dropped the trap.

Hanging was not a quick or kind death in 1862. George Gardner twitched and jerked at the end of the rope for ten minutes. After an hour had passed his body was cut down and taken back inside the gaol to be buried in quicklime in an unmarked plot. It was the end of a long, hot summer of tragedy.

CHAPTER SEVEN

———◆———

THE FENNY COMPTON MURDERS

The art of policing has come a long way since 1863. These days, policemen are trained to deal with all sorts of confrontations and to resolve them rather than make them ten times worse. To some extent they have learnt from experience, and one of those bitter experiences ended up with the killing of Charles Plummer.

Thomas Ricketts was the Parish Constable for Fenny Compton, a small hamlet on the outskirts of Stratford District. He was a local farmer and reputed to have a somewhat short temper and a ferocious dog. On the afternoon of Sunday 18 October 1863, he was walking across his fields with his elderly uncle, Charles Plummer. Charles had spent a lifetime running a farm at Bascote and had now retired to a town house in Broad Street, Warwick, with his wife. All those years of hard work had taken their toll and he needed a walking stick to get about.

Charles and Henry Beere were also out that afternoon. The eighteen-year-old Henry had come over to the next village of Northend to visit his brother Charles, who was twenty-one. The two lads had been to the pub in Fenny Compton and had drunk a fair bit of beer. The brothers had been brought up in Northend. Charles had not done well for himself though; he had a job on Mr Chambers' farm but had been sacked, the latest in a series of short employments. He seems to have had a careless and arrogant attitude and had frequently been in trouble for fighting. In October 1863 he was back at his parents' home, unemployed. His brother Henry was a much steadier sort of character. Even though he was three years younger he had worked on two farms, one in Brandon and one at Cubbington, both of which gave him excellent references for the job he was due to start at Southam on the next day. Indeed, much of the beer they quaffed that afternoon was to celebrate Henry's new job. Perhaps Charles was just a bit jealous of the way his younger brother was doing so much better than his own rather chequered career. Shortly before six o'clock that evening they set off from the pub to walk back to Northend along the footpaths that skirted the bottom of the Dassett Hills.

Thomas Ricketts and his uncle had checked his cows in one field and were walking across the next when they spotted the two brothers weaving a somewhat unsteady path back to Northend. Thomas set his dog off after them. The beast shot across the grass at speed, not even barking. Charles and Henry shouted at it as it closed on them. Hardly surprisingly, they used some pretty ripe language.

Thomas Ricketts thought that they were swearing at him. 'Don't you speak to me that way. Go on.' Charles Beere turned about and asked Thomas who he was and what he had to do with it.

'I am the Parish Constable and the occupier of this land. If you don't go on I will have you taken up for drunkenness.' It was enough to rile Charles Beere. He started to take his coat off. Henry stepped between the two and said to his brother,

'You must not strike him.' Thomas stood on his dignity, and once again told him he was the Parish Constable and would arrest him for being drunk. Charles was getting furious and despite Henry once again trying to restrain him, stepped up to Thomas and slapped him round the side of the head.

Things rapidly went downhill from here. Thomas Ricketts grabbed his uncle's walking stick and knocked Charles to the ground with it. Not content with that, he really laid into him with it, belting him several times as he lay on the grass. Poor old Charles Plummer was standing a yard or two away, unable to get out of the way since his nephew had taken his stick. He wasn't expecting this on his Sunday afternoon walk. He tried to calm Thomas down.

'Don't hit him, Thomas.' Thomas' blood was well up by now, and as Charles Beere started to get to his knees, he hit him with the walking stick so hard that it broke, the crooked end flying off across the field. Charles Beere was knocked to the ground once again. Beaten black and blue by the stick and with a skinful of beer, he was beside himself with rage.

Once the stick had broken the odds between the two men were evened. Charles lurched to his feet and lunged at Thomas Ricketts. The two of them fell to the floor, Charles scratching at Thomas' face and punching as hard as he could. Thomas managed to get on top and grabbed him by the throat. Henry came up and shouted something about fair play, but the two of them were far too busy. Thomas Ricketts seems to have been all set to start a fight and Charles Beere was the sort of person who really didn't need any encouragement to oblige him. The dog seems to have had the most sense of all of them, and ran off.

Charles was starting to weaken and called for his brother.

'Why don't you go into him?' Henry decided that enough was enough; his brother was getting a pasting.

'I can if you like.' And with that he started punching Thomas as well. Old Mr Plummer was far too frail to come to his nephew's aid and shouted at the brothers,

'For God's sake don't kick him!' Thomas Ricketts was definitely getting the worst of it by now. He managed to scramble out from the flailing feet and fists and sprinted off across the field as fast as his legs could carry him. Charles and Henry chased him for some of the way, but gave up at the first stile. Thomas ran on towards the village.

In the field Charles Beere was berserk with fighting fury. He turned back from the fleeing farmer, saw the old man and rushed at him. Henry Beere tried to hold him back but there was no stopping him. Charles Beere knocked Mr Plummer to the ground and started kicking him. Henry grabbed him by the waist and tried dragging him off by force. Charles continued to kick the defenceless old man with his heavy hobnailed boots. Gradually his red rage calmed a little and Henry managed to pull him away. They started to head for home.

Thomas Ricketts ran the few hundred yards to the farmhouse where he met his cousin, William Ricketts. Panting for breath, he explained the gist of what had happened, persuaded William to go back to the field to see if Mr Plummer was all right, and then sent his son to call out the regular policeman. He paused to wash some of the blood off his face. Then he set off back to the field.

William Ricketts climbed over the stile into the field and saw the two brothers, one holding the other about the waist. As he went towards them they ran away. A bit further on he saw Mr Plummer lying on his side in a furrow. He ran up and saw that he was covered in blood.

'Are you hurt?'

'Very much.'

William tried to lift the old man up, but he was too weak to stand. There was blood pouring from a ragged wound on his scalp, more from his mouth. He was in a dreadful state. William shouted for help. Thomas Ricketts and PC Oughton came into the field to find William cradling the old man, his head slumped against William's chest. They gently carried the old man back to the farmhouse.

PC Oughton, together with Thomas and William Ricketts, set off across the fields in pursuit of the two young men. They caught up with them after a third of a mile and the three of them managed to arrest them. The first thing they did was to take them back to the farmhouse for Mr Plummer to identify them. He had now been washed and propped up in bed. He looked at the two brothers; Charles stood rigid whilst Henry was slumped sadly against the wall.

'It was him, the stiff one.' Thomas Ricketts also confirmed to the constable that it was Charles that had fought with him. The constable then took the handcuffed brothers to the Southam lock-up. That night Mr Plummer's condition gradually became more and more serious.

Mr Elkington, the Warwick surgeon, was called on Monday morning, and Mrs Plummer came over from Warwick. Charles Plummer had lapsed into unconsciousness. He had been kicked so hard in the face that the bridge of his nose had collapsed inwards, pushing fragments of bone through his skull, while numerous other wounds on his skull concealed other fractures. Three of his ribs were also broken and one of his teeth knocked out. They were wounds that could have easily killed a young man, never mind an elderly one. He gradually faded through Monday night and died on Tuesday afternoon.

The inquest on Wednesday was held at the Red Lion. The two brothers were brought from Southam and the coroner listened to the various accounts of the affray. It soon became clear that Charles Beere had been the main culprit and since he was still wearing the boots in which he was arrested, these were examined in detail. There was blood and hair on them, the hair matching that of the old man. Both brothers were remanded on a charge of assault and the inquest adjourned for a week so that the men could obtain legal counsel.

This was a bit academic since when the inquest was resumed the next Wednesday neither of them had been able to afford a lawyer. The day was taken up with arguments about whether the inspector at Southam had given them a proper caution before taking down their statements, whether the old man had made his identification of Charles Beere in a sound state of mind, whether he knew he was dying and whether the two brothers had intended to kill him. It was all very technical, apart from a scathing attack on the way that Thomas Ricketts had effectively provoked the two into a fight. It was from that that the whole sorry story had developed. The jury retired to consider what to make of it all.

The verdict of the inquest was that Charles Beere should stand trial for wilful murder, but that Henry Beere should be acquitted. Nevertheless both brothers were brought to trial in December.

The trial saw further criticism of Thomas Ricketts, but dwelt at length on the way that the old man had been kicked in a violent frenzy by Charles Beere. Henry's behaviour as a peacemaker was praised. The question before the jury was whether this was a case of wilful murder; in which case Charles Beere would go to the gallows, or a case of manslaughter. The judge directed the jury to take into account that the brothers had simply gone out for a drink and had not planned any violence at all. Thomas Ricketts' aggressive behaviour had inflamed Charles Beere's own temper and that he had then lashed out at the old man in a drunken fury. The fact that he had subsequently died was not the intention and so the case must be one of manslaughter. Charles Beere was found guilty and sentenced to life imprisonment. It was not to be the last violent incident in the village.

The Oxford Canal meanders past the village along its summit level. Normally canals don't make for very fast getaways, but here on the twenty-two mile summit a boat can be a long way away before anyone has time to count their sheep or cows. Once the railways had driven the canals into economic collapse, there were plenty of very poor boatmen who thought nothing of a bit of poaching and rustling to boost their meagre earnings. You could grab a cow, whisk it up to Birmingham and make some serious money. Unsurprisingly it didn't take long for gangs to get this sort of crime quite organised. The canals of the 1880s were isolated by their poverty and were a very introverted world where strangers were not welcome. They were the perfect environment for such nefarious deeds. It was thought that the boatmen would steal anything that wasn't nailed down, a terrible slander since they would probably have had the nails as well.

Above left: The killing of Charles Plummer stunned the sleepy village of Fenny Compton.

Above right: The Oxford Canal winds through the village and brought all sorts of unsavoury characters on the boats.

Between organised gangs of poachers and pilfering bargees, the police needed a steady and reliable presence in the village. They chose Police Constable Hine as the perfect man for the job. William Hine was born in September 1856 at Ingon, just to the north-west of Stratford. His father was a farm labourer from Halford, near Shipston. His early years were spent at Ingon and then the family moved to Shottery where his father worked on Mr Canning's farm and William went to the local school there. Once he had left school he worked for a while on the railways and then decided to emigrate to Australia. That turned out to be something of a mistake and he returned to Shottery and, after a brief time working on the farm, decided his best career would be in the County Police.

William joined on 9 February 1880. He was a well-built, handsome young man of twenty-three, slightly taller than average at 5ft 9ins and weighing about thirteen stone. He had dark brown hair and eyes and a fresh complexion. His first posting was to Henley-in-Arden in May of that year. Now that he had a steady job he was able to marry his sweetheart, Emily Edwards. William proved himself a capable officer and by November was transferred to Shipston-on-Stour, a somewhat more troublesome spot than Henley.

William and Emily moved into a house in New Street and William soon came up against one of the local poaching gangs. The Batchelor brothers were up to their necks in cattle rustling and other petty crimes. PC Hine had several run-ins with them and they nearly beat him to death at one point, but he persevered with his investigations and eventually had them arrested. They were not best pleased with this and swore that one day they would do for him. PC Hine had received plenty of threats as a result of his duties, and mostly they could be dismissed out of hand. The Batchelor brothers were very nasty characters indeed and he confided to a fellow officer,

'You may depend upon it; they mean to do for me sometime. That will be my end.'
It was probably a relief to be transferred to Fenny Compton at the start of 1885.

The Wharf Inn was the centre of cattle trading for a wide area.

William and Emily now had two sons and as ever with a new house, soon Emily was expecting again. They had a cottage near the church and from this central position William could patrol the village and district, keeping an eye on the various goings-on. Fenny Compton was quite a busy little village. The East & West Junction Railway and the Birmingham & Oxford Railway had stations there, together with a wharf on the Oxford Canal and the main Warwick to Banbury road not far away. There was a regular cattle auction at the Wharf Inn and livestock came and went from quite a large district. The Wharf Inn, or the George & Dragon as it was sometimes known, had something of a dubious reputation. Lights were often seen burning late into the night, long after the ten o'clock closing time. Boats from London and Birmingham quietly moored up, fed and groomed their horses and were away again before anyone knew what their business was. PC Hine had his work cut out.

By the start of 1886 PC Hine had become the established village bobby of Fenny Compton. He had annoyed the local crooks and kept a close eye on the cattle markets held at the Wharf. One of the miscreants, James Plester, had already threatened him but he was nowhere near as nasty as the Batchelor brothers and William discounted this as idle beer talk. The weather that year was dreadfully cold and that in itself cut down the amount of crime as everyone stayed indoors by the fire.

On Monday 15 February there was a cattle auction booked at the Wharf Inn and PC Hine was given discretionary duties for that day. The following day he was due to go to Warwick and help out at the races. For most of the day he stayed at home helping his wife with the children. However, he decided to have a walk around the village in the evening. He put on his full uniform and heavy greatcoat and set off around nine o'clock. The village seemed quiet enough so he took a walk along to the Wharf Inn and arrived there at half past nine. Mr Joseph Hardman, the landlord, offered him a sandwich and the two of them chatted for about ten minutes. As they were eating a couple of the customers discretely left. They were James Plester and Ben Hill, both of whom had been helping at the auction that day. William then popped out and checked the wharf and nearby buildings before going back in just before ten. It was closing time and the last few punters were finishing their drinks. Zephaniah Brown and Blick Reading finally left to walk home towards Farnborough. PC Hine bade goodnight to the landlord and started his walk homewards. He was never seen alive again.

In the darkness of that cold night, shortly after ten o'clock, a young lad at the mill and an older man called Oliver Grub heard scuffling noises and suppressed screams. Miss Emmott heard them too, but thought they were just ordinary drunks playing about. Several people saw a horse and trap being driven at speed through the village, although that was hardly a rare occurrence.

Emily Hine waited up for William for a while, but decided he must have got a lift over to Warwick for the next day's races. Early on Tuesday morning the Ettington policeman, PC Prime, arrived at the house. He too was expected to help at the Warwick races and thought he would walk the rest of the way with William. Emily told him that she thought he had been given a lift the night before. It seemed a bit odd to PC Prime but he said nothing until he got to the race meeting and found that William was not there. Deeply concerned, he told Inspector Hall and once the fuss of the races died down, several officers set out for Fenny Compton.

They started a brief search that afternoon. There was no sign of PC Hine at all. Their fears were raised more when Thomas Knight handed PC Prime a stick that he had found in Cotterill's Field. It belonged to PC Hine.

By Wednesday the whole village was searching for the missing officer. Rumours were flying round that he might have run away, perhaps to Australia. The police had already considered this, but decided it was unlikely. William's life savings of £30 were still safely in the bank, and anyway, he had already visited Australia and hated the place. His pay was due to him on the Tuesday, so Monday night would have been a pretty daft time to abscond.

The local farmers all started to search their fields for any trace of him. By half past nine, the butcher found some ominous signs in his field beside Wharf Lane. The turf was all cut up and scuffed about as though there had been a ferocious fight. He looked about and soon found something even more sinister. About twenty yards away a policeman's helmet lay upside down in a ditch, with a handkerchief beside it. It had been there for a while; already there was rainwater inside it. He picked it up and noticed a long straight dent in it. He quickly called the searching police to the scene.

Superintendent Hinde and the other officers searched the field intensely. There had clearly been a fierce fight where the scuffmarks cut into the turf and leading off from these were some marks of something being dragged away. At the end of these marks lay a huge pool of blood soaked into the grass. The helmet was found about two yards from this ghastly puddle. It was beginning to look as though PC Hine had been murdered. The dent in the helmet suggested that someone had used a club or stick to knock him down and he was then overpowered in a fight, knocked out and dragged closer to the hedge to be despatched. The bloodstained turf was dug up and sent to Dr Bostock Hill in Birmingham for analysis.

Thursday saw the police searching the field and nearby ponds. There was a deep pond close by and they dragged that all day, but without finding anything. The search was extended to the Burton Dassett hills and as far away as Ettington and Shipston. They were now looking for a body, although some of them still hoped that William had simply run away and would be found alive and well. Sergeant Stone, the officer from Kineton, was instructed to interview William's parents in Shottery. William's father was furious at the suggestion that his son might have run away. He told the sergeant that he was sure William had been murdered and his body disposed of in the limekilns at Harbury or in the canal nearby. He told them that when William returned from his journey to Australia he had sworn he would never go abroad again. William's family were distraught at the thought of their son being murdered, saying 'he was as good a lad as ever broke bread'.

Mr Gibbons, an Ettington farmer, lent a pair of bloodhounds to the police, but by now any scent had gone cold and the dogs spent the whole of Thursday traversing the area towards Northend to no avail. They were handed back on Friday morning. Time was passing and the longer it took to find the body the longer the murderers had to make their getaway. The Chief Constable, Mr Kinchant, started to put the pressure on to the local police, and on Saturday the 20th he came down to join the search, along with his deputy, Mr Moth.

With the Chief Constable present the search started all over again, with a lot more attention to detail this time. Almost immediately they found a twin-bladed pocket-knife in the brambles close to the pool of blood. The shorter of its two blades was open and the whole knife was covered in blood. The search carried on over the weekend, with particular attention given to pools, ponds and the canal. Nothing else was found.

The limekilns on the Harbury Road were examined. They had been unattended on the Monday night and if a body had been thrown in, it would have been completely consumed in the immense heat that turned limestone to a dry powder. There was no sign of any interference with them and proved another blank. The name of James Plester came up quite promptly and officers were despatched to search his house and interrogate him. For a while it looked as though they may have got their suspect.

Plester had threatened PC Hine with violence and on searching the house where he lived with his parents and brothers, they found bloodstained cloths and freshly laundered trousers. The trouble was that all three of the Plester brothers worked at the local brewery and had good reason for washing their trousers so frequently. It was a filthy job. There was also a satisfactory reason for the bloodstained cloths and the men had alibis. There was no reason to pursue the matter with them any further.

On Monday Mrs Hine was asked to identify the pocket-knife. It hadn't had the blood cleaned off it. She simply fainted. With this dramatic confirmation, it was also sent to Dr Hill for analysis. Rumours of more cattle rustling kept reaching the police. Mr Boddington complained two of his cows went missing on the weekend before the murder. Everyone was sure it was a murder now, despite the body not being found. On Tuesday the owners of the canal were informed that the police wanted it closed the following day for dragging, and if necessary they would want it drained. The local foreman arranged for stop planks to be sent up so that temporary dams could be put in place at various bridges.

The dragging commenced early on Wednesday morning at the Wharf Inn. It was a long and tedious process, pulling a rope backwards and forwards across the width of the canal, gradually working along one step at a time. Officers had been brought in from across the county, some working on the draglines, others in plain clothes scouring the district. Eventually, after a quarter of a mile, at two o'clock, the line caught on something. PC Lowe tugged hard and suddenly a body floated to the surface. It was quite clearly PC Hine. The spot was on the outside of a bend, the very deepest part of the canal. Whoever had dumped the body there must have known the canal. It was nearly half a mile from where the fight had taken place.

The body was moved to the Wharf Inn for the inquest. PC Hine had not been robbed; all his money, watch and notebook were intact. His watch had had stopped at six minutes after eleven. A watchmaker was called to examine it and he thought that it may have run down rather than been stopped by immersion in the canal. Superintendent Hinde was not convinced; he knew that William made a habit of winding it up in the evenings. The real horror of William's fate became clear as the post mortem continued.

He had suffered a heavy blow to the head as well as quite a lot of bruising. There was a single knife wound in his throat, only half an inch wide. This wound went directly into his jugular vein, and had been twisted so that it was much larger inside than out. He had been killed in almost exactly the same way that a pig would have been. There was no sign that he had drowned in the canal and Dr Thomas Elkington determined that William was probably dead from loss of blood before he was thrown in the canal. A further post mortem was carried out on the Thursday with two more doctors present. The Warwick surgeon, Mr Alfred Lawson Heale, was not so certain that the wound in his neck was the cause of death, since the loss of blood from the vein wouldn't necessarily be enough. When PC Hine was recovered from the water his fists were clenched and there was mud inside his fists. He had no water in his lungs however, so this conclusion remained tentative.

PC Hine's body was eventually recovered from the canal at this point.

On Friday 26 February the inquest was held at the George & Dragon. The circumstances of PC Hine's disappearance and discovery were detailed and Doctor Elkington then gave his evidence:

> I think he must have been held over something and then stabbed, the same as they would kill a pig... It was the most scientific way to kill a man, and if the most skilful anatomist in England had tried to do it he could not have done it better.

The inquest verdict was that PC Hine had been murdered by person or persons unknown. The hunt was now on for a ruthless killer, or even a gang of them.

William's body was taken to Stratford for his funeral. The weather had really set in now and there was over 18ins of snow on the ground. It took no less than three horses to draw the hearse to Stratford. Thousands of people lined the route and packed Holy Trinity for the service. He was then laid to rest in the new cemetery on the Evesham Road. Although there was no official provision for Emily, his widow, the County Police force allowed her a year's salary and a public subscription raised more funds to help her.

The problem for the detectives was that the long delay between the murder and the discovery of the body had let the trail go cold and the criminals make their escape. James Plester had come up with an alibi and when the Batchelor brothers were interrogated they too had managed to have watertight cover stories. Try as they might, there were just no other avenues to research. They just had to hope that someone would come forward with information. It seemed clear that PC Hine had either interrupted a cattle-rustling gang, or he had been the victim of a revenge killing. Only an experienced butcher would have killed him in that cruel manner.

A reward of £250 was offered for the apprehension and conviction of the killer. This brought forward a woman called Alice Corbett, who informed the Dudley Police that an acquaintance of hers had told her that he had something to do with it. Samuel Mountford was a boatman by profession and she swore that he had said to her:

> Goodbye Alice, I shan't be here much longer in this country. I shall have to scamper, for I am mixed up in the Warwickshire job, that policeman's murder, and there's more than one in it, so it's sure to come out.

The Dudley Police wasted no time in arresting Samuel and he was brought into Dudley Magistrates Court on 15 March. He was a complete nervous wreck; this was a hanging offence. Samuel Mountford was a twenty-three-year-old boatman, only just over 5ft tall with black hair and grey eyes. As the trial progressed, it turned out that he had courted Alice Corbett's sister and there was a strong suspicion that she was out

THE FENNY COMPTON MURDER.

DISCOVERY OF THE BODY.

The search for the body of Police-constable Hine, of Fenny Compton, whose sudden and mysterious disappearance was reported in our last issue, was resumed on Saturday morning last, when an important discovery was made by the police. It will be remembered that Police-constable Hine, who had been stationed at Fenny Compton for eighteen months past, suddenly disappeared on the night of Monday, the 15th inst., and since then, up to the time of writing, his whereabouts have remained a mystery, although the search has been persistently pursued by a large contingent of police, assisted by two valuable bloodhounds, lent by a gentleman who resides in the district. On Saturday afternoon a close search was being made by Mr. Kinchant, chief constable of Warwick-

It soon became clear that the policeman had been ruthlessly executed.

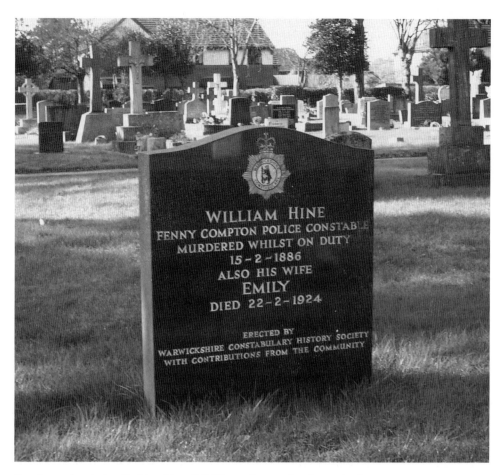

Despite a subscription for his widow, PC Hine only got a headstone in the 1990s.

to get even with him. The case collapsed under allegations that the Dudley court did not have the power to charge him over a Warwickshire offence, that Alice was being vindictive, and a general lack of evidence. Samuel Mountford was kept in custody as the trial was adjourned. The Warwickshire Police came up to interview him and make enquiries amongst his friends in Dudley and the Black Country. It seems that at one point he tried to cut his wrists as the relentless pressure to confess mounted up. In the end though, there was no evidence at all to implicate him and he was released.

There the trail went completely cold. Despite the reward, no one else came forward and the years passed. To this day the crime remains unsolved. Emily never remarried and was eventually laid to rest in the same grave. PC Hine was not forgotten though. In the 1990s, members of the Warwickshire Police Historical Society published an account of the terrible events of February 1886 and raised funds for a memorial headstone so that PC Hine would not be forgotten.

CHAPTER EIGHT

—◆—

THE MYSTERY OF GEORGE TIMMS

'The Devil tempted me to it!'

Some murders have a dreadful sense of inevitability about them. Going through the old records, every now and then one comes across the phrase, 'Well if I can't have her then no one shall', and you just know it's all going to end in tears and blood all over the place. However, some murders just appear like a bolt from the blue. There's no signs or clues to suggest anything out of the ordinary and suddenly – wham, it's time to redecorate. After researching over 200 cases for my various books, such incidents are rare and perplexing. There was one case at Kingstanding where Edwin Thick suddenly killed his wife whilst she was asleep, chopped her into bits and hid them in the cavity wall. They were a devoted couple to all appearances and had only just moved into their new house. In researching this book I was keen to see if anything similar had happened in Stratford. The closest I came was that of the Emscote Tragedy, and the parallels are positively chilling. Moving house is supposed to be stressful, but this takes the biscuit.

George Timms was a fifty-three-year-old engineer at the Nelson Works in Emscote. He had been a steady, sober and reliable workman there for over a decade. He was trusted to work on the prestigious new project, the Filter Machine, and his bit of the factory was called Timms Shop. He was even offered one of the new row of houses being built for the best workmen in the brand new Charles Street. His wife, Harriet Fanny Timms, was a nurse and the two of them had been married for twenty-eight years, raising two sons and a daughter, latterly at a house in Avon Street. It was a bit cramped since their oldest son, Henry, was sharing the house and had a wife and two children of his own. During December 1887 they must have watched the construction of the new houses in Charles Street with interest and anticipation. George and Harriet were to have the first one, and Henry would stay in the house in Avon Street with his new, and no doubt noisy, family.

Something was not quite right. George had always been such an affable fellow, cheerful and pleasant to get on with, but during that December some of his workmates noticed a change. Some days he would lose his temper in the workshop and throw his tools down violently, or stand around morosely not talking to anyone. Other days he was fine. His workmate Boswell could make no sense of it at all. Even when he was in a right mood and flung the spanners around willy-nilly, he was still perfectly civil and quietly spoken. The local shopkeeper noticed that his behaviour was changing as well, becoming more and more reticent, sometimes coming into the shop and then wandering off again. Overall however, there was nothing serious to raise anyone's concern.

On Sunday 15 January 1888, the new house was ready and George and Harriet started to move their furniture in. Like any newly-built house, the builders hadn't quite finished; the walls had yet to be painted, the fender around the bedroom fireplace was just a loose set of bricks and the locks were still a bit stiff, but eager to get a bit of peace and quiet in their own house, they moved in anyway. There wasn't a huge amount to shift. In the kitchen was a table, two high-backed chairs, a large oil lamp and a box of plates and crockery. There was Harriet's workbox (a tin Chocolate Cream biscuit box) with her sewing things and spectacles. Upstairs was even more sparse, with the main bedroom containing little more than the bed, a small table with an oil lamp, and a candlestick on the mantelpiece. The popular image of Victorian houses being cluttered with all sorts of ornaments is all very well for the middle classes, but if you worked in a factory, life was an altogether more spartan affair.

Henry made sure that they settled in, although Harriet was concerned that the new street had no lights and people wanting to call on her assistance as a nurse would be frightened of coming up such a dark road. Still, it was close to Nelson's Mills where George worked and some of his workmates were moving into the new houses at the same time. Things would no doubt get better as the new community grew.

On Wednesday George walked down to work with George Woodfield, his new next-door neighbour and workmate of some fourteen years. At lunchtime they walked back home together, George Woodfield commenting on the cold damp weather. After work they returned to Charles Street together once again. George commented on how it had dried up, but was colder.

'I think it'll be a cold one tonight. My eye, how the wind comes across from Dickins.' The new street seemed to be prone to an east wind. It all seemed perfectly normal, nothing could have prepared George Woodfield for the ensuing night.

Henry Timms came round to see that his parents were settling in. He brought his two young children with him and they played on the floor whilst George and Harriet sat in the high-backed chairs each side of the kitchen range. Henry stayed with them from a little after six o'clock until half-past seven that evening. As he was getting his coat on to leave, his father complained he just couldn't get warm, which struck Henry as a bit odd since the kitchen range was well stacked with coal, the bedroom fire was alight upstairs and there was plenty of coal in the shed. Harriet said he would probably feel better when the new order of coal was delivered. George seemed to be in a funny mood. Slightly perplexed, Henry took his children back home.

Above left: The house in Avon Street was too small for three generations of the Timms family.

Above right: The Nelson Works was the largest employer in Warwick. It produced gelatine in vast quantities.

Silence settled over the new houses as the night darkened. George Woodfield vaguely remembered hearing a few sounds as George and Harriet settled down. The walls between the houses were rather thin. He rolled over and went to sleep. Warwick gradually became quiet as the night advanced, and by midnight the streets were deserted save for the regular police patrol.

PC Salt was on duty, walking along the top of Smith Street. He greeted Edwin Harris with a cheerful 'Good morning' as Edwin walked up from The Butts on his way to his job at the fire station. Nothing out of the ordinary there. The clock was striking one.

Suddenly there was a commotion at the bottom of Smith Street. Someone was shouting and banging the doors. Salt ran down the road to see what on earth was going on. George Timms was staggering across the street, reeling about as though he was drunk and shouting at the top of his voice. As PC Salt approached, George yelled, 'There he is!' Salt grabbed George but he wrenched his way out of the policeman's grasp. 'I have murdered my wife. The Devil tempted me to it!'

George was making such a racket that Edwin Harris heard it from the other end of Smith Street. He ran down to where PC Salt was struggling with the hysterical George Timms. Timms threw himself onto the ground. The constable tried to get him to answer to his name, but could get no sense out of him.

'Have you been home?' managed to get the answer 'Yes' as Timms hurled himself across the road again. Edwin Harris asked the policeman if he wanted help. He did indeed. Together the two of them managed to subdue him and half drag him to Warwick Police Station. PC Salt handed Timms over to the duty officer, PC Lewis.

'He has stated he has murdered his wife.' They laughed. It seemed too bizarre and anyway, Timms appeared to be blind drunk. Timms seemed to finally notice where he was; 'Yes, you will find her there; you will find the back door open.' he said quite soberly. Then he carried on lashing about in hysterics.

The sixteen new houses in Charles Street were built to the most modern standards of the time.

The two policemen looked at each other and then at Timms. In the lights of the police station, Salt suddenly realised that there was blood all over Timms' hands. Indeed, the skin was ripped open on one of his left fingers. There wasn't the slightest smell of alcohol on Timms. They called PC Durham to assist in getting him into the cell.

PC's Salt and Durham were dispatched to check what had happened at the house. Luckily, Edwin Harris knew that the family had moved into the new house that week and told them exactly where to go. It was all a mystery; everyone knew that George Timms was a sober, hard-working fellow who had never been in any sort of trouble before. The two policemen talked it over as they made the mile-long walk to Charles Street. He couldn't really have murdered his wife, could he? It was impossible to believe.

The front door was locked, but the back door opened when they tried it. It was all dark except for the faint glow of the kitchen range. PC Durham lit the small oil lamp on the kitchen table. Everything looked normal at first. There was a white cloth on the table, a cup and saucer that still had a bit of tea in the bottom and Harriet's workbox.

PC Durham noticed that there were spots of blood all over the lamp he was holding. They went upstairs with a sense of deep foreboding. The one bedroom was empty, but the second…

Harriet lay face down on the bed. She was in her nightclothes, half the blankets fallen off but looking quite peaceful. Her right hand was at the back of her head and the left just under her left cheek. As the policemen's eyes adjusted to the dim light, they realised that the back of her head was a mass of blood, there was blood splattered up the wall by the bed and there was even blood on the candlestick on the mantelpiece on the other side of the room.

They checked her wrist for a pulse, but there was none. Her hand was quite cold even though her body was still warm. PC Salt looked about and noticed the bricks around the fireplace were slightly out of order. He picked up one; it was covered in blood and hair. The two policemen backed out of the room and PC Salt ran back to the station to summon a surgeon and raise the alarm. PC Durham waited in the empty house with only the sound of the blood dripping off the saturated pillow for company.

Inspector Hall started to question Timms whilst Dr Rankin returned with Salt to the house. Timms was still very nervous, although he could now answer to his name and state where he lived. He jumped back as the inspector went to search his pockets.

'The Devil tempted me to it.' The inspector warned Timms that whatever he said may be used as evidence and Timms finally started to calm down. When Inspector Hall told him that Harriet was dead, he just answered,

'Is she?' He then made a statement that read, 'We had some words after going to bed over some trouble. I hit her with a brick two or three times. Something shot through me when I was in bed. I have had no rest since I have been there.' The inspector told him he would be charged with her murder and he replied, 'If I have done it, I am very sorry.'

The next week was a busy one for the police, but they found nothing that could explain the sudden murder. Many of Timms' workmates said how he had been acting a bit queer in the last few weeks, but there was nothing that could explain the 'trouble' that Timms had alluded to in his statement. He was little help to the investigation, as he seemed unable to recall anything of the actual deed itself. Timms was an emotional wreck by now, alternating between floods of tears and a kind of stunned remorse. 'She was all my love during our thirty years of married life.'

Harriet was buried the following Monday as the committal hearing for George's trail was taking place. The meagre facts of the case were examined in detail, but still nothing explained the sudden lethal outburst. Henry Timms stated that he had never heard an argument between his parents. When asked if his father had ever shown signs of violence towards his mother his answered 'No, never, never, never.' The mystery simply deepened.

The *Warwickshire Advertiser* conveyed the shock of the whole town at the bizarre killing.

The case came to court at the end of July. George Timms pleaded not guilty. Appearing in the dock he presented a sorry sight, broken and dejected, his face wet with tears. He watched nervously as his counsel, some of the best lawyers in the Midlands, proceeded to give the judge several reports as to his sanity. His first trial had been adjourned so that these reports could be compiled. All the newspapers had been full of speculation as to what had happened. Had he been sleep-walking, was there some inherited madness? Psychology at the time was in its infancy and the whole affair was most disturbing. Could anyone be suddenly afflicted in the same way?

The jury decided that George had been insane when he committed the murder, and was therefore innocent of wilful murder. They also judged that he was criminally insane and should therefore be detained at Her Majesty's pleasure. George Timms was to spend the rest of his days in an institution, a broken wreck of a man.

CHAPTER NINE

—⸻◆⸻—

THE GAMSENFELLS ENIGMA

One of the strangest and most puzzling murder cases ever to happen in Stratford is that of Johan Lachmann von Gamsenfells. To this day, the precise motives for his actions are shrouded in darkness and mystery.

Johan Lachmann von Gamsenfells was born in Bohemia in 1850. He left this small German state after serving as an artillery officer in the Austrian Army during the late 1870s and moved to London. In those days London was home to political exiles from all over Europe. In the succession of wars and revolutionary movements, England became home to characters like Karl Marx and all manner of communists, socialists, royalists, anarchists and nihilists. Our government kept a vague eye on their activities, but allowed them a surprising degree of freedom. London became home to hundreds of political newspapers of every nationality and political belief. Johan Gamsenfells had trained as a print compositor and shortly after arriving in the teeming metropolis put his printing skills to good use. He started the *Londoner Journal*. This was a weekly German language newspaper that aimed to keep the various exiles in touch with current events back home. Its main topics were politics and finance, both of vital importance as Bismarck forged a bunch of principalities into a united Germany. The paper was founded in February 1878 and Johan was the editor on a salary of £3 a week. This was a very good wage for the era; it enabled him to marry Rosanna Halls of City Road and not long after she bore him a baby boy. He managed to get the financial backing of a Mr Probat so that although he was no longer in sole charge, at least he had secure backing to keep the paper going.

Matters may have ended there, just one more political exile making a new life for himself in a strange country. Unlike the French Communard exiles, there was no hope of an amnesty and a return to the homeland. The Bohemian community in London were stuck with little hope of return as the new Germany became stronger. Johan Lachmann von Gamsenfells wanted more from life than that of an exile.

Although an editor of a magazine, Johan Gamsenfells was very shy and retiring at work, so much so that not even Mr Probat, the newspaper's owner, actually knew where he lived. In fact he now lived with his wife Rosanna at No. 2 Louisa Cottages,

Forest Gate. Their domestic life seemed perfectly normal, although she was often left alone for days or weeks at a time as he worked hard collecting material for the paper from all across Europe.

Only once were Rosanna's suspicions raised about her husband's fidelity. In 1884 she found a letter. It was probably a love letter, but she couldn't read the German text. Instead she went around to the address and told the woman, one Caroline Menthey, that Johan was a married man and to keep her nose out of her family. As far as she was concerned, that was the end of the matter and Johan gave her no more cause for concern; there were no more letters. Mr Probat knew of a different story. Johan had an aristocratic air about him and used this to charm many of the young German girls that he met in London. He was an accomplished musician as well, and was a popular guest with the other German families. He played the zither so well he could reduce people to floods of tears as he evoked the tunes of a homeland that many would never see again.

It was around 1884 that Johan met another woman who opened up new horizons for him. Madame Hercules, as she was known, was an entertainer, able to sing and play the zither well, and perform astonishing feats of mind reading. The two of them seem to have fallen passionately in love. She was about twenty-three-years-old and also originated from Germany, although no one was certain as to precisely where from. It was only a matter of time before Johan was spending a lot more time 'at work' and told his wife it was more convenient to stay overnight at the office in Brown Street rather than commute all the way to Forest Gate. In a matter of months he had rented a small apartment for his new girlfriend and started leading a complex double life. Madame Hercules was now expecting a child.

Mrs Freeman ran a boarding house in one of the cottages along the Tiddington Road.

Despite widely circulating a picture of Madame Hercules the police never managed to identify her.

Even though £3 a week was a good salary for the time, it was not really enough to support two separate families. Johan's savings were gradually eaten up and after a couple of years matters started to get very difficult indeed. He started to reduce the money he gave Rosanna, and Madame Hercules was subjected to the indignity of several moonlight flits as they sought to keep ahead of the rent man. Although Rosanna lived in a normal household, Madame Hercules had barely a stick of furniture to call her own. She and Johan decided to try and make some extra money by going on the stage, playing the zither and performing a mind-reading act. After a few false starts in London, in 1888 they performed in Ostende at Christmas and the following year they spent the summer on the Isle of Man. By now she had a little girl called Maggie to look after as well. She managed to get some friends to look after the child whilst she was away.

The two of them gave a series of concerts at the Salisbury Hall under the names of Herr Mozart and Madame Lenormand. The alias of Lenormand was taken from the very famous French tarot card reader, Marie Ann Lenormand, a woman who read the cards for the French revolutionaries like Robespierre and royalty like Czar Alexander. In her day she was the most famous tarot card reader in Europe. The *Manx Punch* for July 1888 gave them a very good review and described how Herr Mozart played the zither impeccably and that Madame Lenormand had a pure and sweet voice. After the music recital,

Herr Mozart went down into the audience and performed a mind reading act. He took random articles from the spectators and the blindfolded Madame, with her back to the audience, accurately guessed what the items were. The reviewer was thoroughly impressed. The landlord of their lodgings was not in the least impressed. He had lent Johan the money for the hire of the hall and the concerts had not really made enough cash to pay him back. Johan returned to London, leaving Madame Hercules to try to make up the shortfall with a few more concerts. This didn't work and she returned to the city leaving a large trunk as security for the money. Some weeks later Johan sent the cash to the landlord, together with the cost of sending the trunk back to the office in Brown Street.

The spring of 1889 passed with several more changes of address for Madame Hercules, but Rosanna's household remained stable and normal. Johan was often away for weeks but Rosanna was able to keep in touch with him by letters to the office. It may seem a little odd to us today, but in late Victorian times letters and postcards were the equivalent of text messages, and virtually as quick since postal sorting and deliveries in the city were extremely efficient. You could literally send someone a letter inviting them to lunch that day and receive a reply before laying the table. In early July, Rosanna received a letter from Johan saying he was going away. She sent their little boy round to the office to get some housekeeping money from Johan before he left. Johan gave him 17s 6d. Nothing seemed out of the ordinary.

Financial pressures were piling up for Madame Hercules though. A woman answering her description registered at the Soho Servants Registry Office looking for work as a domestic servant. This woman gave her name as Lina Monthey and her previous employer as Mrs Gamsenfells. Alas, this Mrs Gamsenfells was in Paris so couldn't provide a reference. The Reverend A. Fleming interviewed her and decided to offer her a job. However, just a couple of days later this Lina Monthey called at his house and told him she couldn't take up the post since she was engaged to be married and would be going abroad. It is possible that this Lina Monthey was one and the same person as Caroline Menthey who signed the love letter back in 1884. Matters were certainly getting complicated.

By August Johan decided a short holiday was in order. On the 13th he told his printer foreman that he would be away for a couple of days, but that he would be back on Friday to get the paper ready for publication. Madame Hercules, the little girl Maggie and Johan boarded a train from London to Towcester and then took the East & West Junction Railway to Stratford, alighting at the New Street Station in the late morning of Thursday 15 August. They walked into town and took lodgings at Mrs Freeman's house on the Tiddington Road. The house was close to Clopton Bridge and overlooked the river. Their initial idea was to stay only one night and return to London by the late train on the following day. They had not brought much in the way of luggage with them. Mrs Freeman thought that they were a pleasant married couple and that Maggie, the little girl, was utterly cute. She took the little girl round to Mrs Jones who ran the shop on the corner of Shipston Road, where she played whilst Mr and Mrs Gamsenfells walked around the town sightseeing.

On the Friday Johan paid Mrs Freeman for their lodgings and said they had intended to catch the train but would rather spend longer in town. Indeed by four o'clock in the afternoon they came back and asked if they could stay on until Monday. Mrs Freeman had no other bookings, and so they went back into the same first floor room. That evening the little girl, Maggie, was left in the room while Johan and his mistress walked around the town, calling in for a drink at the Old Red Lion. There had been nothing in their manner to arouse Mrs Freeman's suspicions. The woman had told her that she was a concert singer and from Germany. She also told the old lady that she was very much in love with Johan. Both of them seemed fond of the little girl. Over dinner the two of them had spoken in German, so Mrs Freeman had no idea what they were talking about, but the tone and manner of their conversation seemed normal enough.

Saturday dawned bright and sunny. All three of them went out for a walk around the town and out as far as Anne Hathaway's cottage. Here Madame Hercules picked a rose from the garden and put it in her purse as a keepsake. Although Johan was a striking man, tall, dark-skinned and with a magnificent large Germanic moustache, few people remembered seeing the family on their walks. That evening they went into the Shoulder of Mutton pub but made no effort to speak to another German man staying there. They returned to their lodgings reasonably early and put Maggie to bed. They spent a while talking with Mrs Freeman. Johan wanted to show her how he could mesmerise his wife, but she said she didn't feel up to it. Then they did their magic tricks, with the blindfolded Madame Hercules successfully guessing cards drawn randomly from a pack. Mrs Freeman wasn't daft and accurately spotted that the words Johan used as he drew the cards were a special code that gave away the value of the card. Still, it was all harmless fun and a staple of family entertainment in the days before everyone spent their evenings comatose in front of the television.

Sunday followed a similar routine except that after lunch with Mrs Freeman, they left the little girl at Mrs Rose's shop whilst they went for another walk. In the late afternoon they called to collect her and Mrs Rose invited them into the back of the shop. Here Mrs Rose's daughter played 'Home Sweet Home' on the piano, and Johan corrected her timing so that when she played it again Madame Hercules sang the accompaniment. She then followed this with a very moving French song. The two of them then gave an impromptu magic show that quite astounded Mr and Mrs Rose. Madame Hercules could even divine the number of blades on a penknife without seeing it. It was all very cosy.

At about nine o'clock the family returned to Mrs Freeman's. Johan seemed very withdrawn and dull. He didn't speak a single word, which struck Mrs Freeman as a marked contrast to the night before. She asked them if they would like some tea but they both said no. Then Maggie said she was hungry and hadn't had anything since lunchtime. Madame Hercules said she shouldn't have anything as it would stop her sleeping, but then relented and asked Mrs Freeman for a couple of slices of bread and butter, saying that she would pay for it in the morning. The old lady got the bread and butter together with a drink of brandy and water. The family retired to their room.

On Monday morning, a little after eight o'clock, Mrs Freeman started to get breakfast ready in the kitchen. She could hear a man's footsteps upstairs in the bedroom and assumed that the Gamsenfells were waking up. A very loud gunshot rang out, moments later there was another, quieter, one. Mrs Freeman ran to the bottom of the stairs and shouted out. 'What is that noise?' There was no reply. With her heart racing, she ran around to the house next door and told Mr Jones that she thought her lodgers had shot themselves. Mr Jones said he would get a ladder to look in through the window, but Mrs Freeman told him the blinds were shut. She was in a dreadfully agitated state by now and Mr Jones ran to call the police whilst their son was sent to find a doctor.

Luckily, as they were running across Clopton Bridge they met PC Price and PC Northam together with Mr Mather, a pharmacist. They all rushed back to the house. Upstairs the bedroom door was locked, but PC Price started to batter at it with his shoulder. A whimpering sound from Mrs Freeman made him redouble his efforts. There was blood dripping through the ceiling downstairs. As the door burst open a terrible sight greeted them.

Johan Lachmann von Gamsenfells was curled up on the floor in a large pool of blood. A revolver lay beside his left hand. In the bed lay his mistress, lying on her right side, and just behind her lay the little girl. Both looked asleep, apart from the blood all over their faces. They had both been shot in the left temple. Each one of them was still breathing very faintly but even as the officers checked, Johan and his mistress died. Mr Mathers tried to rouse the girl and washed her wound with some cool water, but she was too badly wounded and died half an hour later without ever regaining consciousness.

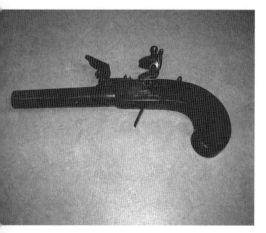

Above left: The single shot pistol was only a small calibre weapon, but lethal to a child at close range.

Above right: The revolver was still warm when they broke down the door.

Superintendent Charles Simmons arrived and started to try to make sense of the bizarre scene of carnage. It appeared that Johan had woken up and taken a single-shot pistol in his left hand, and a five-shot revolver in his right, and then shot his mistress and daughter in a single instant as they slept. The single shot pistol lay on a chair and was still warm when the officers arrived. He then sat on the floor and used the revolver on himself. The bullet from the revolver passed right through his mistress's head and lay on the pillow, whilst the bullet he used on himself lay on the floor. The bullet that killed Maggie was still lodged in her head, as the gun was much less powerful.

The room provided few clues for the detective. There was no suicide note or other obvious clue. The door and windows were locked so it seemed clear that no other person had been involved. Through the morning he assessed what few clues he did have. The family had a suitcase with a few clothes and some posters advertising their Isle of Man and Ostende concerts, together with press cuttings. There were a few personal bits of jewellery and business cards, there was a bunch of keys with an 'If Found' tag on them and a free press pass for the Spanish Exhibition in London, but ominously the detective found only one halfpenny coin. The family had no other money at all. Outside a crowd gradually grew as news raced around the town.

During the rest of the day Superintendent Simmons searched the room while the bodies were washed and laid out on the floor. He had little success in finding any clue to the identity of the woman and girl. There were a couple of photographs in the case, one of Johan and one of the woman, with the words 'Madame Hercules' written on the back. The business cards at least gave Johan's work address and the superintendent telegraphed the Metropolitan Police to start an investigation in London. There were a few personal letters amongst the woman's possessions and since these were in German, he asked a local schoolteacher to translate them. Unfortunately they contained no useful information.

It was all very unsatisfactory. Mrs Freeman was still in hysterics and was being cared for next door; she couldn't bring herself to go back into the house after seeing the blood dripping through the ceiling. The Superintendent sent letters to the company named on the key ring and to the proprietor of the Salisbury Hall in the Isle of Man. By Tuesday morning, when the inquest was called, he had still not had any response. The jury was sworn in and with no more information available to the police, they inspected the scene of the crime and then took testimony from Mrs Freeman. They then adjourned the inquest and gave permission for the bodies to be removed for burial.

What followed showed Stratford in a very poor light indeed. The Clerk of the Board of Guardians refused to accept liability for the cost of their burial, stating that the cost had to be borne by the person on whose premises they died. This was the still traumatised widow Mrs Freeman, who certainly couldn't afford the burial. The clerk, Mr Warden, stuck to his position, stating that the Poor Law Union would be surcharged at the next audit if they paid. The bodies were left lying on the floor of the house until Wednesday. Mr Kneller, the owner of the freehold, then lodged a complaint with the Sanitary Office that the bodies created a nuisance by not being buried, but the inspector, Mr Brook, visited the house and decided that this was not the case. Sharp words were exchanged, but Mr Brook then obtained the support of the District Medical Officer, who merely recommended that some disinfectant be spread in the house.

The deadlock was broken in the early hours of Thursday morning when Mr Ainsworth, the Relieving Officer of the Poor Law Union, took the responsibility for the decision himself, saying that in all humanity he could not just leave the bodies lying there. He felt sure that all reasonable ratepayers would endorse his decision. He instructed Mr Kibler, the undertaker in Tiddington, to prepare three coffins. Once he had broken the deadlock, the Chairman of the Board of Guardians then backed him up, rather than face the growing public outrage.

Money, or at least the lack of it, was to continue to plague the affair. The Metropolitan Police had traced Rosanna Gamsenfells and she had written to Superintendent Simmons saying she would not be able to afford the train fare to be able to come and identify the body of her husband. She said that it was almost certainly him, although she had no idea who the woman or child were. Superintendent Simmons applied for the cash for the train fare from the parish, but was refused. He then offered to pay the cost himself. Rosanna arrived by the first train on the Thursday morning. Charles met her at the station and they walked down to the sealed up house. Here Rosanna confirmed that the dead man was indeed Johan Lachman von Gamsenfells, but she point blank refused to even look at the woman and child, stating that she knew of no relationship between her husband and any other woman. She did look at the woman's photograph, but said she had no idea who she was.

The keyring proved to belong to Mr Probat, and his evidence was next to useless; he couldn't even provide names of any of Johan's friends, let alone any clues about the woman and child.

The true identity of Madame Hercules was to remain a mystery. Despite a thorough investigation by the London Police, no firm identity could be ascertained. They found out that she had lived at 6 Gore Street on a couple of occasions, but every other lead met a dead end.

On Thursday afternoon the three coffins were taken to Alveston Church. One had a smart brass plaque naming Johan, but the other two were blank. In the burial register they were simply stated to be an 'Unknown woman and child'. Alveston Church was packed with people from Stratford, but even so the Reverend W. Barnard absolutely refused to say the burial service over Johan's coffin since he had committed suicide. He did however perform the service for the woman and child. All three were buried beside the wall of the church. Several floral wreaths were sent, one with a card that stated 'With deepest sympathy for the poor little girl'. Mr Kibler's children made up another wreath of weeping willow surrounding the now faded rose that the unfortunate woman had picked at Anne Hathaway's cottage. It was a very melancholy affair indeed.

Alveston Church is the last resting place for Johan Gamsenfells and an unknown woman and child.
There is no headstone.

The inquest was resumed in September. No more evidence could be produced to identify the mysterious Madame Hercules and the motive for the crime was just as obscure. The majority of the jury decided that Johan had snapped under the financial pressure of trying to run such a deceitful double life. At the conclusion of the inquest the jury set up a fund to collect money for Mrs Freeman, and managed to raise nearly £20 for her. The coroner then stated that since the jurors had been called on three occasions he would award them a triple fee, and the jurors then donated this fee to Rosanna Gamsenfells. Superintendent Simmons was warmly thanked for his efforts and the coroner recommended that the parish should reimburse him for his expenses in paying for Rosanna's train fares and other costs. An official curtain was then drawn over the whole sorry story.

No one in court mentioned the presence of a woman who had waited outside the fatal house for several days after the shooting. Quite a few locals, who thought that she was Johan's wife, had noticed her. She was still there when Rosanna came to identify the body, so the gossip turned to other alternatives. The police were informed and Superintendent Simmons tried to find her, but she vanished into the crowds, and, try as he might, he couldn't apprehend her. Rumour had it that she was at the burial service, but in the milling throng of spectators the police couldn't find her. She clearly wasn't a local woman. Was she connected to that other German gentleman staying at the Old Red Lion? Was there something more to the double murder and suicide than just poverty? The two guns that Johan used were expensive pieces of equipment, and could easily have been sold for the equivalent of a week's wages. Despite the Metropolitan Police investigation that included circulating Madame Hercules's photograph to Germany as well as all over London, especially in the German ex-patriot community, nothing was found at all. The ex-pats simply closed ranks and said nothing. Given that Johan was involved with a political newspaper, perhaps there was far more at stake. History however holds its secrets very close and we will probably never really know what events led up to that horrific scene on the Tiddington Road.

CHAPTER TEN

—◆◇◆—

THE GHASTLY END OF HANNAH BROWN

Ely Street has never managed to become a prestigious address in Stratford. Despite being right at the heart of the town it has housed some of the worst slums and the most dubious characters throughout the town's history. The events of 1895 simply confirmed what everyone already knew – it was a pit of depravity and sin.

Walter Wheeler was a pleasant enough chap by all accounts. He was short and slim, generally polite and inoffensive. When he was twenty-three, in 1889, he married Ann Huckfield. She was a twenty-eight-year-old dressmaker who already had a child by her first marriage. They first moved into a very squalid set of rooms at No. 4 Garrick Court and then into No. 15 Ely Street. Ann gave birth to Samuel in 1890 and another child in 1891. This youngest child died after only a few months. Within a year or so, Ann had had enough of Walter and walked out, leaving him with the two surviving children, Charles, his stepson, and Samuel, still a toddler. Walter was left in a difficult position, having to raise two children on his very meagre wages as a labourer. He desperately needed a partner to help out.

Mrs Hannah Brown should not really have been Mrs Brown at all. A few years previously a town scandal erupted when it turned out that her previous husband, Mr Hurst, hadn't died at all but was alive and well and living as far away from her as he could get. She had married Mr Brown bigamously and he promptly chucked her out onto the street to fend for herself. She was then prosecuted, fined and lived in what was described as very 'wretched circumstances'. She met Walter Wheeler and moved in with him, ostensibly to look after the children. She was twelve years older than Walter and a very generously built woman. The only cloud on the horizon was her penchant for beer, and lots of it.

So the small Walter Wheeler and the extremely stout Hannah Brown started their somewhat tempestuous domestic life. Once she had a few beers on board, the whole street could hear the rows and arguments. Walter was comparatively kind to her despite all this and she never complained about him at all. The children were cared for and everyone hoped that Walter would make an honest woman of her. If only life could be so simple.

Monday 14 January 1895 started off as usual. It was a bitterly cold day with snow lying on the ground. Walter went off to work, and Hannah packed the kids off to school and spent the morning doing the chores. By lunchtime she was feeling a mite thirsty and went out to get some beer. By mid-afternoon Charles and Samuel came back from school and she sent Charles off to get another jug of beer, and then another, and then another. Charles may well have been learning his maths at school, but he soon lost count of the times she sent him out for more beer. At about four o'clock Hannah wobbled off down the road to speak to Mary Ann Pryor in No. 17, and Mary noticed that she was decidedly the worse for drink. Hannah returned to her house and sent Charles out for yet more beer.

Shortly before seven o'clock, Walter returned home and found Hannah absolutely plastered. Presumably this was the last straw for him, as his account of the subsequent events is rather different to everyone else's.

Out in the street a young lad by the name of Albert Ward was just finishing work at No. 48 and walking past. He heard a 'disturbance' and stopped to listen. There was shouting and what sounded like a 'lumping' noise, as though someone was chopping wood. He went back into the house and waited for a few minutes before coming out again. The noise had finished and he saw Walter sweeping water out of the front door as though there had been a flood. Inside Albert heard someone moaning and Walter called in and told them that he would conduct himself better if he was her. Albert was sure that Walter was speaking to Mrs Brown. He hurried off to his home on the Birmingham Road.

Mary Ann Pryor also heard a 'bumping' noise at much the same time, as did Mary Ann Bliss, another resident of Ely Street. They all seemed to think it sounded like chopping wood. It wasn't.

Once called Swine Street, Ely Street has never been a wealthy part of the town.

THE STRATFORD TRAGEDY.

Walter Wheeler, 31, labourer, of Ely-street, Stratford-on-Avon, was indicted for the manslaughter of Hannah Brown at Stratford-on-Avon, on January the 14th last.—He pleaded not guilty. —Mr. Carter prosecuted, instructed by Mr. S. C. Warden (Messrs Warden and Son, Stratford).— The first witness for the Crown was Mary Ann Prior, who lives in Ely-street, and was a neighbour of the prisoner's. She had seen the woman in the afternoon, when she had evidently had some beer. Later in the day there was a "bumping sound" heard in the prisoner's house, and presently Wheeler came running into her house, saying, "Come into my house; I can't make anything of my Betty." Witness went and found her lying on the floor, her clothes being saturated with water.

Above: The *Warwickshire Advertiser* reported the sorry tale.

Left: Hannah sent her son out to get her more and more beer.

Charles and Samuel arrived back and went into the suddenly silent house. Charles found Walter throwing a bucket of water over the unconscious body of Hannah. She was lying on the floor near the fireplace and it seemed that Walter was trying to wake her up. He went out to the yard to get another bucket of water from the half-frozen water butt. Walter told the two boys to go up to their bedroom.

A few minutes after seven o'clock, Walter rushed out of the house and down to Mary Ann Pryor's, telling her that he needed her help.

'Come into my house, I can't make anything of my Betty.' Mary went in and found the house in a terrible mess. There was broken crockery scattered all over the place and water all over the floor. Hannah was slumped on the floor, soaked through with freezing water. She now had a black eye and there was blood coming out of her nose.

'She is dead.' Mary told Walter.

'Never, never, fetch a doctor!' Mary told him to get one himself as she tried to get Hannah up onto a chair. Walter ran out into the street and bumped into Henry Worrall. He gave some kind of garbled account to him and raced off to Doctor Henry Ross. Henry Worrall went to the police station. Mary shouted for another neighbour, Mrs Hodgkins, to come and help. As it was, Hannah was just too heavy for anyone to lift.

PC Flockton arrived with Henry Worrall soon after this. Doctor Ross had already examined Hannah and pronounced her dead. She appeared to have a serious bruise and possibly a fracture on the back of her head. Her face had clearly received several blows as well. The policeman asked how this had happened and Walter told him that she was terribly drunk when he got back from work, and when she tried to get up out of the chair, she had slipped and banged her head against the wall. She had grabbed the tablecloth as she fell and dragged the crockery onto the floor as she went. PC Flockton was not convinced. There was a drop of blood on Walter's face and there was more on the walls near where she lay. He looked closer and found spots of blood on the table and on the other walls at about 5ft from the ground. He arrested Walter on suspicion of manslaughter.

As darkness fell, Walter was taken to the County Police Station and Doctor Ross sealed up the house for an inquest the next day. The two young boys were sent to their grandmother's house. The whole town was buzzing with the gossip.

On Tuesday morning Walter Wheeler was brought to the Town Hall and PC Flockton gave evidence to the Mayor, Mr Smallwood. Superintendent Lambourne and Sergeant Kendrick applied for Walter to be remanded in custody until Thursday, which was granted. An inquest was called for the Wednesday. There seemed to be a lot of sympathy for Walter's plight. Hannah Brown, with her history of drunkenness and bigamy, was clearly not one of the deserving poor, whilst the hard-working and inoffensive Walter clearly was. His story that she had fallen over because she was so drunk tallied with what most people knew of Hannah, and even if he had punched her a couple of times, well that was no more than she deserved.

The inquest on Wednesday morning soon showed how deeply held this prejudice ran. Dr Ross had not conducted any further examination of the body. He accounted for the black eye as the result of a 'tiff' because she was drunk, and the bruising to the back of the skull a result of her falling off her stool. He had treated her for various ailments before and thought that she would have a weak constitution due to the drink. He didn't mention the possible effects of three buckets of ice-cold water being poured over her.

Walter elected to give evidence himself, even though the coroner cautioned him to be careful. He gave a clear and concise account of how he found her very drunk, and how she fell over and banged her head, pulling the crockery off the table as she went. He spoke of how he tried to revive her with the water, and then called for help when that failed. The jury were impressed. In fact they were so impressed that several of them suggested that a post mortem would not be necessary. The coroner was not quite so happy. The doctor had not really supplied a clear cause of death and this was not good enough. He requested a post mortem, nominally so that Walter Wheeler could be cleared of the charge of manslaughter. The inquest was then adjourned until the results of the post mortem were available.

That afternoon Dr Ross, together with Dr Arthur Haydon of Harley Street in London, conducted a detailed post mortem. He soon found that there were far more extensive injuries than he had first supposed. The wound on Hannah's head had not fractured the skull, but it had caused severe internal bruising. Hannah's legs were covered with bruises, and her right leg was broken just above the ankle. He concluded that these bruises and the break were caused by 'great violence', but were not individually enough to have caused her death. However, the extent of the battering she had taken, coupled with the shock of several buckets of ice cold water being thrown over her was quite sufficient to have given her heart failure. He said that the 'lumping' sounds that people heard may possibly have been the sounds of Walter kicking her. He then qualified that by saying that the sounds might have been caused by Walter sweeping the water out of the house with a short bristled broom. Dr Haydon agreed with this conclusion. Although they tried to avoid it, the conclusion had to be that Walter gave Hannah a terrible kicking, punched her in the face twice and that she then bashed the back of her head as she fell over when her leg was broken. He may well have tried to revive her with the water, but it proved to be the final straw for her weak heart.

Above left: Ely Street has never been short of pubs; in Hannah's day there were four.

Above right: The inquest was held at the Town Hall.

The coroner gave permission for Hannah to be buried on the Friday, and the inquest resumed on the Saturday. The post mortem results were conclusive and Walter was remanded in custody on a charge of manslaughter. The case would be heard at the next Warwick Assizes. The jury donated their fees to the children's grandmother who was still looking after them.

The March Assizes were unusually quiet for a change. The sessions opened with an address by Baron Pollock. In his preamble to the various cases, he outlined the case of Walter Wheeler who he described as a 'respectable character', unlike his 'paramour' who had ' given way to habits of intemperance'. The case had all the elements of a life ruined by the demon drink.

Walter pleaded not guilty, but the prosecution made out a good case that he had caused her death by the assault. In Walter's defence, Dr Ross gave evidence that he had treated Hannah for various ailments concerned with her drinking and that these had weakened her. He thought that an ordinary person would not have died as a result of such an attack. The jury retired to consider the matter for a few minutes. They returned a verdict of guilty, but with a recommendation for mercy. The judge, after a lecture on how even the drunks of this world should be treated with kindness, sentenced Walter to just eight months' hard labour.

To get an idea of how this sentence compared to others that day, Charles Twist was found guilty of stealing a couple of hundred pheasants from a farm near Alcester and received eighteen months' hard labour, and the chap he sold them to got twelve months. James Shirley of Ettington was found guilty of carving his brother up with a knife and he received a sentence of three months. If Hannah Brown did not have a reputation for drunkenness then Walter may well have faced the gallows, although perhaps then the whole sorry tale would not have happened at all.

CHAPTER ELEVEN

———⊰◈⊱———

UNSOLVED MURDERS OF THE TWENTIETH CENTURY

For some inexplicable reason, Stratfordians were comparatively well-behaved for the first half of the twentieth century. Searching through the archives, records of the previous century turns up a grisly incident at least once a decade, but virtually nothing throughout the first forty years of the next. Apart from the rather bloody affair at Welford Pastures where Mr Robbins used the blunt end of an axe on Mrs Robbins, they were all positively angelic. Maybe they just didn't get caught, or perhaps the slaughter in the trenches of the Somme had put everyone off the idea. It was too good to last and as the Second World War drew to a close human nature reasserted itself with a vengeance.

The murder at Meon Hill has to be the most famous case of all the dastardly doings in the whole history of Stratford. It has got all the elements of a cracking mystery and remains unsolved to this day. It is the archetypal local legend and has just about as much myth woven about it as the stories of King Arthur. If you care to look it up on the internet you'll find all sorts of increasingly fantastic stories, from a witchcraft sacrifice to placate an angry earth goddess to intervention by aliens. By the time you've read most of the stories you wouldn't dream of ever setting foot in the village of Lower Quinton just in case you end up as an extra in a remake of *The Wicker Man*, burnt alive by a screaming horde of six-fingered druids. In fact, the village is a pretty normal place and they don't eat babies at all, ever. Back on the internet you can read how Charles Walton had a cross hacked into his chest by satanic priests to exorcise the winter or how he commanded demons to blight his neighbours' crops. It all gets very confusing, not to say aggravating, for the serious student of history. What on earth really happened, and why all the mystic flapdoodle?

Meon Hill is a pretty odd place. One of the last outliers of the Cotswold Hills, it looms on the horizon of the whole Avon Valley. On its summit are the remains of an Iron Age fort, ditches and mounds left over from an era long before modern man. However, excavations of the fort have revealed no settlement there, and it was probably a ritual site. A cache of iron ingots was discovered there dating back to before the Romans. These ingots were used as currency by the people of the day. It was really hard cash that could be forged into swords when required. The hill has always been treated with a kind of reverence, so perhaps the mystic element was assured from the very start of the investigation. There aren't any stone circles, altar stones drenched in the blood of virgins or even a mythic barrow housing a sleeping army. Those are all down the road at Long Compton.

The date of the murder could also be significant. Valentine's Day, 14 February, has long been associated with pagan fertility rituals. It's the day that the birds pair off for mating and lots of other folklore to do with amorous couples celebrating the spring behind hedges. It must be said that it isn't particularly about sacrificing people to ensure the fertility of the land or the rebirth of the sun; that all tends to be earlier in the year or around May Day when the climate is more conducive to lovers' trysts behind said hedges. Still there's nothing quite like the human imagination to fill out a story. So what actually happened?

On 14 February 1945, Charles Walton went off to work on laying a hedge on the side of Meon Hill and that was the last time anyone definitely saw him alive. By all accounts he was a pretty cantankerous old man. He was seventy-four and had bad arthritis, which would probably account for the cantankerousness. He had always been a farm labourer in the district and was working part-time for Mr Potter of Firs Farm, doing odd jobs to stretch out his pension. He lived with his niece Edith in the village. There was nothing particularly dramatic to note apart from the fact he wasn't well liked in the village.

The village of Lower Quinton acquired a very dubious reputation after the murder.

The day passed like any other and it wasn't until he failed to return home in the afternoon that anyone really gave a thought to him. Edith got back from work at six o'clock and was alarmed to discover that he hadn't come back from work. She persuaded her neighbour, Harry Beasley, to help her look for him, fearing that the old man had fallen and hurt himself. They didn't find him close to the village so asked Mr Potter where he had been working. The three of them walked up to the hedge where he had been. Luckily Alfred Potter and Harry Beasley were slightly ahead of Edith when they found Charles' body. They managed to stop her seeing the full horror.

Charles Walton lay on the ground by the hedge with a pitchfork stuck in his neck and massive wounds to his chest. The bill hook was still sticking out of his ribs. His braces had been broken in the struggle and his pockets were turned inside out. Alfred Potter pulled out the pitchfork and bill hook, but there was no way that he could revive the old man. He was thoroughly dead. He had been struck three times with the bill hook and then, once on the ground, speared through the neck with the pitchfork. Whoever attacked him had made sure he wouldn't get up again.

The local constable, PC Lomasney, was called and confirmed Charles was dead. It was pretty obvious that it wasn't an accident so he called in the County Police. By midnight Professor Webster of the Forensic Laboratory and Superintendent Alex Spooner had arrived to take charge of the investigation. It seemed clear that some absolute maniac was on the loose and Alex Spooner contacted Inspector Fabian of Scotland Yard. He came up from London by the night train.

Daylight the following morning failed to help. The footprints of Beasley, Potter, Edith and the police had obscured anything left by the murderer in the immediate vicinity and any fingerprints on the pitchfork and bill hook had been spoilt when Mr Potter dragged them out of the body. Inspector Fabian ordered a fingertip search of the entire hill by platoons of soldiers co-opted from the nearby Army camp. They even brought their mine detectors to see if any metal had been dropped. Quite how efficient hundreds of squaddies were at searching for clues remains unknown; the whole hillside had now been trampled all over. Inspector Fabian also ordered aerial photographs to be taken by the RAF. It all revealed a complete absence of clues.

The Army camp was also a prisoner of war camp, with over a 1,000 Italian soldiers held there. The security was a complete joke and some of the prisoners used to pop out to go poaching. A plump rabbit was just the thing to stretch out the rather boring rations. One of the prisoners had even been seen the previous day with blood on his hands as he stood by a hedgerow. Nobody bothered about it at the time, which shows just how common an occurrence it must have been. Now it seemed deeply suspicious and the prisoner was identified, blood found on his coat and he was arrested. It turned out to be rabbit blood. None of the other prisoners seemed to have been out that day and they were all accounted for. Another dead end for the investigation. That left the villagers, all 500 of them.

The prolonged interrogation of everyone in the village certainly won Inspector Fabian no friends. He had found a couple of footprints on the hillside and taken plaster casts of them, but this provided no help at all. Everyone seemed to have adequate alibis. Weeks passed and he was getting less and less popular as he stuck his nose into the private lives of everyone in the village. He returned to London and started to write his memoirs.

Quite when the witchcraft rumours started is a bit of a mystery itself. The newspaper reports of the time mention nothing of this nature at all. Inspector Fabian stated in his memoirs that Superintendent Alex Spooner gave him some books about witchcraft as soon as he got off the train. But what senior policeman would automatically suspect witchcraft when there were so many more obvious motives? Inspector Fabian was inordinately proud of his record in solving crimes and it seems to have been him that first mentions the witchcraft theory. Obviously he couldn't be expected to solve the supernatural. Once the rumour of the supernatural forces got out it soon became the accepted theory. Stories of how Charles Walton had seen a spectral black dog, could curse peoples' crops, all sorts of weird stuff soon did the rounds. The pitchfork was supposed to have been the only way to kill a witch and a case was dredged up from the previous century where John Haywood had injured an old woman with one, saying that she was a witch. He went on to threaten another sixteen old ladies in Long Compton and at the time it was generally considered that he was a complete nutter rather than a fearless witch hunter. Naturally, it became common knowledge that the old man had had a cross carved into his chest with the bill hook, despite the local papers accurately reporting the autopsy, which clearly stated that there were three vertical blows to his chest.

In February 1945 England held thousands of prisoners of war, and a fair few had escaped. Desperate and starving in an alien country, they lived off the land. Charles Walton had certainly been thoroughly murdered but he had also been robbed of all the money in his pockets. By the time the investigation started the following morning, his attacker could have been forty or fifty miles away – or he could have been tucked up in bed in the village. We will never know.

The other famous unsolved murder in Stratford is the Gravestone Murder of 1954. Luckily for us it has not been swamped by loads of superstitious nonsense and the facts of the case, few though they are, are clear enough. The murderer is still unknown, and quite possibly is still out there somewhere.

Olive Bennett was a midwife at the Monroe Devis Maternity Home in Tiddington. This was back in the days when you could still be born in Stratford; nowadays it's all in a unit elsewhere so that there's no chance of a rival to Shakespeare being born here.

Olive was a diminutive woman, less than 5ft tall. She originally came from Edinburgh and had trained as a nurse, then a midwife. Over the years she had worked in many different hospitals until, in 1953, she was in Malvern. She was forty-five, single, very pious and also had dreadful teeth. It was here that she had a general anaesthetic and all her teeth removed. Perhaps it was the anaesthetic, perhaps a mid-life crisis, but from that day on her personality changed dramatically. Gone was the inhibited, prim and proper lady. She seems to have realised that she had missed out on a lot of fun in life and decided to make up for it while she still had the chance. She moved to Stratford in March 1954 and started work at the Monroe.

Olive soon became well known to the local taxi drivers as she spent her evenings off in the town. It's about a two-mile walk from Tiddington to the town centre. Although the regime at the maternity home was quite strict, with the nurses having to share bedrooms and a night-time curfew, Olive managed to stay out late most nights. She could be found in the bars of the hotels in town, chatting away to anyone who would spare her the time. There were quite a few chaps who could spare more than just the time. Although she was probably treated quite generously by many of her new male admirers, it was a lifestyle that she couldn't afford on her meagre earnings as a nurse. She began to use up her savings at an alarming rate. She was also drinking very heavily.

As March passed into April, she worked her way through the eligible males of the town, and a fair few not so eligible ones too. If the wives of the town had known what she was up to, there would have been trouble. She seemed to have no friends at the Monroe and was increasingly prone to bouts of depression. Not only was she drinking more with each passing day, but now she was chain smoking almost ceaselessly. It seems her personality was breaking down under the strain of this double life.

She tried to convince one of the other nurses, Ann Swarbrick, that she had a regular boyfriend. Ann wasn't convinced and privately wondered whether he was just a convenient fiction to disguise her increasingly promiscuous behaviour. Olive had also confided in the barman at the Crown in Tiddington that she had spent over £200 on drink in the last few months. 'Aren't I a naughty girl?' she giggled. Olive's life was getting out of her control.

23 April 1954 in Stratford passed with all the usual parades and flags as the town celebrated the birth of the Bard. Olive was at work until the evening, and as soon as she could she put on her grey and white coat, brown hat and walked into town. First she had a quick drink in the Red Horse Hotel and then went off around town. The night porter at the Red Horse was certain he saw her outside at closing time – that was the last positive sighting of her. There was a possible sighting of her in the arms of a man beside the wall of the churchyard around midnight and after that, nothing. She never returned to the Monroe Devis that night.

The next morning the sexton found a shoe, a pair of spectacles and a set of dentures on the path beside the river in Holy Trinity churchyard. He called the police and they soon found a handbag floating in the river nearby. It proved to be Olive's. Stratford is a small town, despite the hordes of tourists that had come to see the birthday celebrations. The police were aware of Olive's promiscuous lifestyle and the way her personality seemed to be collapsing. Their first thought was that she had committed suicide and so they started to drag the river beside the scattered remnants of her life.

Dragging a river is no easy task. The grapnel repeatedly caught onto something but couldn't quite get a grip. The water was so murky that they couldn't see whether they had caught a branch or a body. It wasn't until mid-afternoon that they finally pulled Olive's body from the water. It felt as though something had been holding it down. They called out the county pathologist to check that she really had drowned herself. She hadn't.

Olive Bennett had been in a fight, sustained multiple bruises and then been throttled violently. Her throat was completely crushed. There was no possibility of suicide, especially when they discovered what had been holding her down in the water. A gravestone had been pulled up and thrown on top of her body to weight her down. If it hadn't been for the shoes and dentures that she lost in the fight, her body might not have been discovered for months or even years.

The murder investigation started right away, but promptly ran into a mire of problems. Olive had been involved with so many men in the town, many of whom had no intention of ever admitting knowing her, that it was difficult to know where to start. The last sighting of Olive seemed to be very close to the murder scene and was of her with a man only vaguely described as middle-aged, sturdy and with bushy fair hair. It seemed probable that this was the murderer, but the description was too vague to be of much help. The town had been packed with visitors, locals and even the squaddies from the local Army camps. To Superintendent Alex Spooner it rather looked as though she had known her assailant and had done something to drive him into a homicidal frenzy. Had

Above left: The Bard's birthday celebrations were tragically marred in 1954.

Above right: Olive Bennett met her unknown assailant in Holy Trinity churchyard.

Above left: Her body was flung into the river and then sunk with a gravestone.

Above right: Her false teeth, glasses and a shoe were found on the grass the following morning.

she threatened to expose him to his wife, was she trying a spot of blackmail to boost her flagging bank account? Or had she inadvertently picked up some psychopath?

A search of her room produced nothing to incriminate anyone; neither did her diary. Olive's father came down from Edinburgh to identify the body and arrange her funeral at Alveston Church. He could cast no light on the enigma either. As far as he had been aware she had been living her life just as she had always done. He was shocked to discover just how quickly she had gone through her savings in the last few months.

A week after the murder, the police staged a re-enactment of Olive's last known movements and put checkpoints on the main roads and bridges. It produced no new information. The military police interrogated the soldiers in the local Army camps. Few people would even admit to knowing Olive, let alone admit they had seen her on the fatal night. She had come into the town, led a whirlwind life for a few weeks and now was gone. There were far too many guilty husbands who hoped it would stay that way.

Weeks passed with no more information appearing. The police drained the river and found a couple more of her personal effects, a powder compact and her other shoe. They threw no more light on the identity of the killer. Odd rumours of strangers being seen leaving the town that night were pursued but led to nothing. Even the offer to meet her lovers in a confidential setting out of town failed to produce any evidence to the killer. The paperwork now filled a complete room at the police headquarters. Some of it consisted of malicious accusations which, spurious as they were, still had to be investigated. Ominously, another woman had been killed in a very similar manner in South Ruislip. The question of motive remained as open as ever; was there a serial killer out there or was this a crime passionnel? The police redoubled their efforts, interviewing almost every man in the town, visiting all the factories and hotels. No matter what they tried, there just seemed to be a blank wall wherever they looked.

The case remains open.

Other local titles published by The History Press

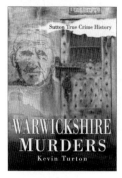

Warwickshire Murders
KEVIN TURTON

From Warwick to Rugby, from Coventry to Nuneaton and from Stratford to Leamington Spa, *Warwickshire Murders* is a powerful and fascinating reappraisal of some of the most brutal and gruesome killings in the county's history, and is sure to appeal to crime enthusiasts. This latest collection explores notorious crimes from the nineteenth and early twentieth centuries, using contemporary documents, trial transcripts and newspaper accounts to examine cases that gripped both the county and the nation.

978 0 7509 4242 3

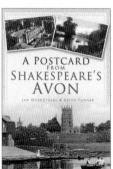

A Postcard from Shakespeare's Avon
JAN DOBRZYNSKI & KEITH TURNER

A companion volume to the authors' *A Postcard from the Severn* and *A Postcard from the Wye*, this book takes the reader on a journey in words and pictures through the five counties traversed by the Avon, using images from more than 250 postcards drawn from the authors' collections – many posted to friends and relatives by some of the innumerable visitors to the river and its world-famous associated attractions. It is a record of how the river and its surroundings once appeared, and how they were immortalised by earlier generations of photographers and artists, printers and publishers.

978 0 7509 4848 7

Murder & Crime: Lincolnshire
DOUGLAS WYNN

These tales from Lincolnshire's forgotten past are testament to the sinister side of the county's coastal resorts and inland market towns. Retold for a new generation are shocking stories of drunken brawls in towns, death from poison and jealous rages. Mixing genuine historical documents with contemporary photography to show the scenes where these disturbing dramas were played out, Wynn's collection of true crime provides a mesmerising evocation of the past. It is sure to haunt the imagination of any reader with an interest in the darker history of Lincolnshire.

978 0 7542 4864 0

Stratford-Upon-Avon and Beyond
JOHN D. OLDFIELD

In this collection of over 200 old photographs and postcards, Stratford and the villages of three counties from the surrounding area are explored. From images of the streets, buildings, pubs and hotels, to the beauty of the river and surrounding countryside, and the development of NFU Mutual – all aspects of working and social life are chronicled.

978 0 7524 0685 5

If you are interested in purchasing other books published by The History Press, or in case you have difficulty finding any of our books in your local bookshop, you can also place orders directly through our website
www.thehistorypress.co.uk